NATURAL GARDENS
Gardening with Native Plants

Natural Gardens
Gardening with Native Plants

By JACK KRAMER

Drawings by Michael Valdez
and Charles Hoeppner

CHARLES SCRIBNER'S SONS
New York

BOOKS IN THIS SERIES BY JACK KRAMER

Hanging Gardens
Water Gardening
Miniature Plants Indoors and Out
Garden Planning for the Small Property
The Natural Way to Pest-Free Gardening
Gardening with Stone and Sand
Ferns and Palms for Interior Decoration
Your City Garden
Grow Your Own Plants
Gardening Without Stress and Strain

Contents

Introduction: YOUR OWN SANCTUARY   ix

1. RETURN TO THE WOODS   3
    Our Native Plants
    Take Notes
    Kinds of Gardens

2. PLANNING AND PREPARING THE GARDEN   11
    Preparing the Plan
    Woodland Gardens
    Woodland Plants
    Bog Gardens
    Bog Garden Plants
    Wild Flowers in the Cultivated Garden
    Plants for Sunny Sites
    My Native Gardens

3. GETTING PLANTS   31
    Seeds
    Other Propagation Methods

4. DETERMINING FACTORS: TEMPERATURE,
MOISTURE, AND SOIL   39
    Soil
    Native Plants for Different Situations
        Trees—Wet Locations

Trees—Dry Locations
Shrubs—Wet Locations
Shrubs—Dry Locations
KNOW YOUR WEATHER
HARDINESS

5. WILD FLOWERS   48
    MORE WILD FLOWERS
    BULBS

6. TREES   67

7. SHRUBS   83

8. VINES AND GROUND COVERS   99

9. FERN GARDENS   109

10. ORCHIDS   118

11. KEEP IT BEAUTIFUL   123
    MAINTENANCE
    INSECT PREVENTION

12. NATIVE PLANTS IN TERRARIUMS   129
    WOODLAND PLANTS TO USE
    FERNS

APPENDIX:
    Plant Sources   139
    Books to Read   140
    Where You Can See Native Plants   142
    Conservation Groups   146
    Agricultural Extension Service   146

Introduction:
Your Own Sanctuary ✒

If you were a city child, a day in the forest preserves was a special treat. It was here you saw your first wild plants and realized that green is not just green. Nature's world of ferns and mosses, trees and shrubs ushered you into a new, and for me, a fascinating sanctuary. For the rural child, such plant treasures were taken for granted but soon missed when the city called or as progress and the bulldozer approached.

Some ten years ago, I bought a home in Northfield, Illinois (thirty miles from Chicago). The one-acre site where the house stood was originally a forest preserve. Fortunately, the house was placed to preserve the site (as much as possible) as it was originally. Here was a natural feast of flowers. I added garden hybrids, of course, but basically, the natural garden that had been there for years remained and was far easier to cultivate than my cultivated plants. And in the spring, the beauty of woodland plants was breathtaking to visitors and myself as well. It was here after thirty years that I renewed my interest in trilliums that were ankle-deep in my back yard! It was here I found long-lost Jack-in-the-pulpits showing elegant flowers under the deciduous trees in the rear of the property. Dogtooth violets blazed along the driveway so thick they were absolutely lush, and willowy may-apples were a canopy of green next to the garage. Now, in California, part of my property too includes a native garden for I wouldn't be without one after my Illinois experience.

For most people our native plants were the first ones they knew, and lovelier plants are hard to find. While cultivated and formal gardens ruled for years, today the woodland or natural garden is a visual treat that kindles forgotten memories. These gardens are no more demanding and perhaps easier (once established) to care for than a strictly cultivated landscape.

There is little doubt that the plants we loved best as children can be grown by us as adults no matter how small the property might be. The beauty of native plants is hard to ignore and their rediscovery by young and old is gratifying. Too long we have depended on improved varieties of foreign plants and abandoned our own American wild plants. However, I am not advocating a dismissal of gardens as we know them. I have written several books about them and practice what I preach. In essence I am saying use all kinds of plants in your garden with a special eye for natives. Learn to use yesterday's plants for they are very much a part of today's heritage. Create a sanctuary for them and for you.

Jack Kramer

NATURAL GARDENS
Gardening with Native Plants

1. Return to the Woods ✍

Our recent interest in nature is long overdue. A respect for our native plants years ago might have thwarted the dismal path we followed in the last two decades and might have prevented today's sorry ecological state. Forests and fields are not as plentiful as they were in my childhood, but thanks to conservation groups and public action, more protected sanctuaries may be in the offing. And protection is necessary; from our wild plants we can learn much about how to improve our personal gardens as well as how to improve our world environment. Because nature has a systematic order—a reason for the smallest insect or flower—we should learn to respect the soil, the plants, and the land. We should imitate nature rather than take from her. And what better place is there to observe plants than in your own garden? Collecting or buying wild species does *not* deplete our natural flora; gardening with native plants is a very real way of preserving them. Be careful, however, to leave untouched all plants on your local, state conservation list.

Thus, the preservation of wild plants should not be only the conservationists' concern. Laws and restrictions on collecting plants will not completely solve an already deplorable problem. *You* must help so that your children and their children will get an appreciation of

OPPOSITE: *Native shrubs, trees, and wild flowers combine to present a beautiful picture in this site. Some plants are in a wet situation, others in sun, each grouping has been selected for appropriate conditions; thus the garden thrives.* (Photo by Ken Molino)

3

nature's beauty for years to come. If native sanctuaries vanish (as they might), at least you will have done something to preserve part of our native land.

Our Native Plants

Even from the very beginning of America's history, plant collectors from other countries sent specimens of our native plants to their lands while American settlers all but ignored our rich harvest of plants for ornamental attraction. (The same is not as true now, although to some extent it is.) Ironically, the American pioneers began importing European plants to use in America.

This anomaly can be explained because we were interested in setting up a new nation and were in no position to do experimentation; civilization and the struggle between life and death was immensely more important. There wasn't time to appreciate the wonders of nature or to enjoy the flowers; other things like hunting and building took precedence. Gardening is essentially a leisure pastime, and there was little leisure in the settlers' days. Also, our country was settled by a potpourri of people with European manners and customs, so they looked to their homelands for their crops, fruits, and even ornamental gardens.

As America became settled, pioneers continued to grow European plants, and our natural heritage of plants was sorely forgotten until recently. Yet quite logically native plants are easier to tend than plants that come from other countries. By nature they are tough, resilient, and eager to live, and they thrive in habitats they are accustomed to.

Foreign species and hybrids need to be tested for several years to determine whether they are going to make it in our conditions. Hardiness and resistance to disease and insects must be observed. On the other hand, because our native plants have been around for a long time, the weaklings and incompetent have already been weeded out. The plants we find here have gone through the survival of the fittest. In other words, they have already been thoroughly tested and have survived.

There are practical reasons too for using the trees and shrubs and wild flowers that naturally thrive in a *specific* locale. To grow an Eastern native in the West can certainly be tried, but California wildlings in the East invariably perish—climatic conditions are just not right. You are trying to establish a garden that will maintain itself over the years, so stress plant material that naturally belongs in that part of the region. Other plants can certainly be used if you are the adventurous type, however. Some natives like mahonia can be grown anywhere in our country. Others, such as the California poppy, are restricted to a given area; we shall discuss many such plants in the following chapters.

Take Notes

If you observe where native plants grow naturally, and simulate and understand these conditions in your garden, you will rarely have failures. Walk through woods and fields, and take mental and written

While this landscape is shaded woodland predominantly, there are wild flowers in sun in the rear; a totally natural landscape is created. (Photo by Molly Adams)

Sun filters through this natural garden, shade in other places in this natural garden where natives and hybrids grow. (Photo by author)

notes as to where and how plants grow, because this will help you when it comes time to start your own sanctuary. Take a small wild-flower guide with you to help you identify plants (see Appendix). Certain plants, e.g. ferns and Jack-in-the-pulpit, grow together in shady nooks; others, like asters and butterfly weed, revel in open sunshine. Plants like marsh marigolds exist in a rich mucky soil, but others are content to grow in a poor sandy base. Observe the color of plant leaves, because it is a key to how much sun and heat a plant needs. Glossy yellow-green plants such as ceanothus thrive in hot, dry places in full sun. Wood sorrel (oxalis) and various dark green ferns prefer a shady moist nook, as do rhododendrons. In between the dry and the moist habitat are plants with medium green lustrous leaves: *Arbutus unedo*, camellias, and azaleas.

I don't mean to say that the plants mentioned *must be* grown in exactly duplicate conditions; they'll survive outside these conditions, but it will require more work and time on your part. Any plant you put in your garden will grow satisfactorily if it is climate adaptable and if you can provide the proper conditions. If the plant freezes and is killed by the first winter, quite obviously it is not wise to grow it— choose instead from the many other available plants.

Kinds of Gardens

Woodland gardens, with their graceful ferns and shade-loving plants, are immensely popular and provide a delightful, cool retreat; they are unique landscapes for many shady sites. For a sunny area there are wildlings that can add great color too, and immeasurably decorate the property. Furthermore, flowers of the field are the easiest to grow and generally can fend for themselves. Spiderwort and lilies, goldenrods and iris, sumac and yuccas are all good possibilities for the sunny garden. Wood lilies and wild orchids are also delightful and fanciful flowers you may otherwise never see because wild stands of these plants are now almost extinct.

A bog or marshland garden is another little-known or infrequently seen scene; this site will open the door to a whole new world of fascinating plants. The bog plants are dramatic and impressive and we should use more of them in our landscapes. Tiny marsh marigolds (*Caltha palustris*) with dark green leaves and bright yellow flowers are an effective example of nature's beauty. The blue-flag (*Iris versi-*

This site is marshland or bog in nature; ferns and lovely foliage plants abound.
(Photo by Molly Adams)

color) is stunning along the perimeter of a small pond. Mixed with lush green arrowheads (Sagittaria) they offer an enchanting scene. Some bog plants can be used in the woodland garden too if soil is moist; I am thinking of the grass pink orchid (*Calopogon pulchellus*) which I have grown successfully in my garden.

A fern garden is another fine scene with lush growing plants in different tones of green. Some ferns appear almost emerald in shade, others are deep green and still others almost apple-green. And ferns once established grow lavishly with almost no care. There are few plants that can match the grace and beauty of our native ferns. So if you have a neglected shady spot or a forgotten cranny on your property where you think nothing will grow, by all means try some ferns. They will transform the area into a green wonderland. Hundreds of ferns are available for your gardening pleasure, and we list many of them in Chapter 9.

2. Planning and Preparing the Garden 🌿

Variations in climate, soil, and temperature are part of our vast country's geography. For example, in California you can be in entirely different climatic conditions if you travel five or ten miles; the same (to a lesser degree) is true in other parts of the country. Each geographical area has its own variations, and these factors will determine what kind of native garden to have.

There are plants for all conditions. Once you start you'll realize that native plants are no more demanding than other garden subjects and that they may, in fact, be easier to grow. For example, wildlings can pretty much fend for themselves once they are established (don't forget that they have been doing it for thousands of years). Give these plants the proper location and they will take off on their own, although in the beginning there may be fatalities. Observe and experiment; it's half the fun of cultivating wildlings. You know what to expect from garden hybrids, but wildlings are an adventure, and you'll find yourself entering a whole new role of gardening, one that is immensely satisfying.

PREPARING THE PLAN

Before you start, know your property; this is as important as knowing your climate. The easiest way to begin is to make a rough plan on paper. If your contractor has given you a plot plan, draw the outline of your property. If you have no plot plan, walk your property with tape measure and record the dimensions and shape.

Mark North, South, East, and West on the sketch, and put in existing plant materials. Be aware of the shade patterns existing trees

11

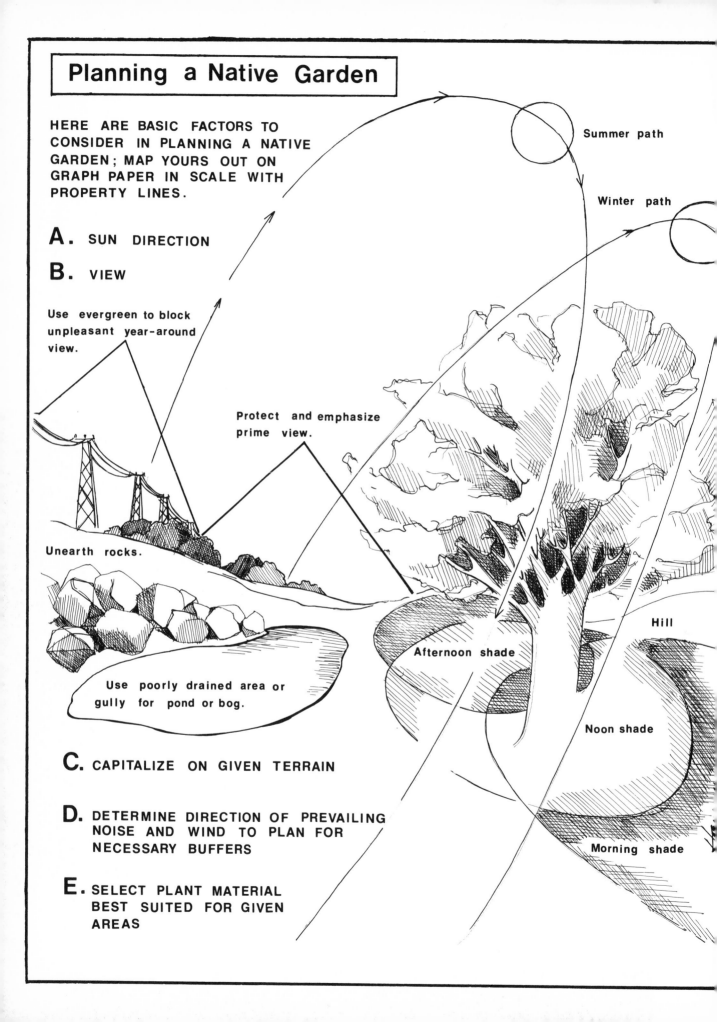

Planning a Native Garden

HERE ARE BASIC FACTORS TO
CONSIDER IN PLANNING A NATIVE
GARDEN; MAP YOURS OUT ON
GRAPH PAPER IN SCALE WITH
PROPERTY LINES.

A. SUN DIRECTION

B. VIEW

Use evergreen to block
unpleasant year-around
view.

Protect and emphasize
prime view.

Unearth rocks.

Use poorly drained area or
gully for pond or bog.

C. CAPITALIZE ON GIVEN TERRAIN

D. DETERMINE DIRECTION OF PREVAILING
NOISE AND WIND TO PLAN FOR
NECESSARY BUFFERS

E. SELECT PLANT MATERIAL
BEST SUITED FOR GIVEN
AREAS

Summer path

Winter path

Hill

Afternoon shade

Noon shade

Morning shade

create. If the sun and its angles confuse you as much as they do me, study the drawing so you'll know how the sun strikes your property; it is *immensely* important. Also consider the prevailing winds for different times of the year. Make note of dry and wet areas; ferns, for example, will succeed in the moist cool areas but never in the dry unshaded places. The natural contours of the land are also important. Seek out intriguing levels for eye interest. A garden should never be monotonous, and grade changes handled cleverly can be more moist at the bottom of a hollow than at the top of a crest.

If you follow the dictums of your garden's topography and conditions, the natural elements of good design will fall into place too;

Native trees and shrubs make a lovely frame for a small house; nothing is manicured or formal, and still the view is appealing. (Photo by Matthew Barr)

SOUTH EASTERN WOODLAND GARDEN

plants will look as if they belong to the land rather than just planted. The totally naturalistic garden is a garden that, although freshly planted, appears as part of the property and provides a totally captivating picture.

Woodland Gardens

On an average site there will be a place for a woodland garden. It may be a small island between shade trees, or if the area is larger, you can mark out paths that are surfaced with pine needles or wood chips. Provide an acid and rich humusy soil; if it is sandy, watering will be a problem. Sources of humus are rotted sawdust or decayed wood chips, leaf mold, or any decomposed materials.

Set woodland plants in natural groups. For example, trilliums, American columbine (*Aquilegia canadensis*), and various types of ferns always grow in colonies. Creeping phlox (*Phlox stolonifera*) with its mauve flowers is stunning, and the leathery green leaves of wild ginger (asarum) are a handsome garden accent. Solomon's seal (polygonatum), with creamy white bells in spring and handsome blue berries in fall, is another good wild plant, and, under trees, *Galax*

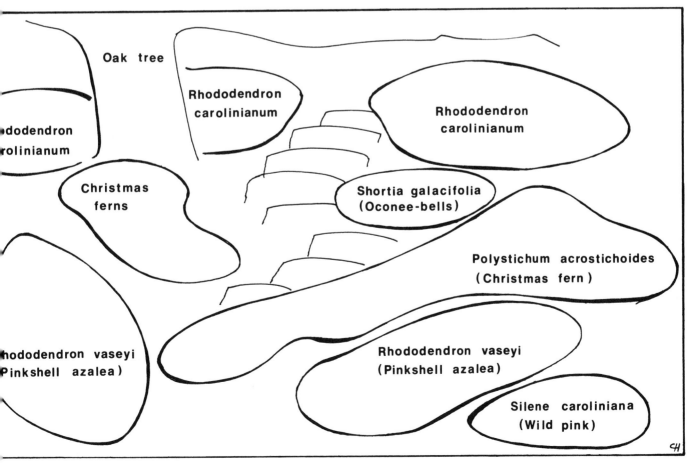

KEY TO SOUTHEASTERN WOODLAND GARDEN

aphylla, with white wands of flowers and beautiful foliage, grows like a weed.

Trees, of course, play an important part in your garden. If at all possible, never remove a tree, unless it is diseased or in irreparable shape. Rather, prune lower branches, but always remember that filtered sunlight should strike the garden site. Remove underbrush and seedling trees, and along with wild flowers use native trees and shrubs like oak leaf hydrangea (*Hydrangea quercifolia*), native viburnums, and sweet pepperbush (*Clethra alnifolia*). Native rhododendrons, heaths, and azaleas offer immense color and are available from several sources. The common Eastern shrub *Kalmia latifolia* (mountain laurel) grows to ten feet, with pink to white flowers in May and June. A smaller laurel (*K. polifolia*) will also grow in the rich soil of the woodlands; the blossoms are pale to deep red.

There are dozens of beautiful azaleas (rhododendrons) that can enhance a woodland garden. In the East, *Rhododendron nudiflorum* and *R. roseum* (sometimes considered a variety of *R. nudiflorum*) are favorites, as is the fragrant and lovely swamp azalea (*R. viscosum*). The flame azalea (*R. calendulaceum*) is native to the Middle Atlantic states and extends south to Georgia and Alabama. The beautiful pinkshell azalea (*R. vasevi*) is indigenous to western North

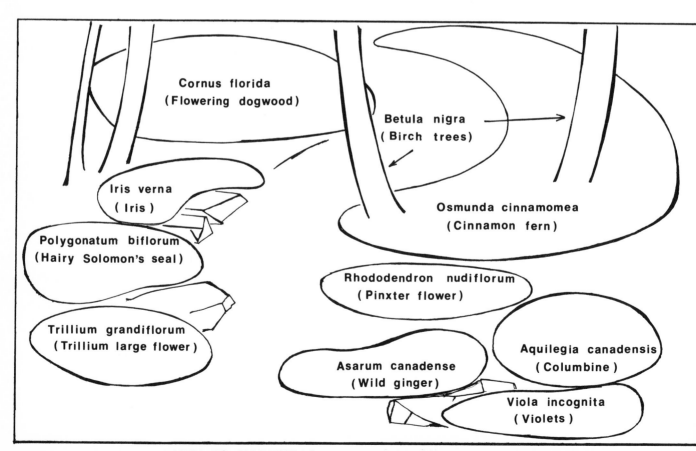

KEY TO NORTHEASTERN WOODLAND GARDEN

NORTHEASTERN WOODLAND GARDEN

MIDWEST NATIVE GARDEN

Carolina but hardy as far north as southwestern New England. The largest and perhaps best-known azalea is *R. maximum*, an upright shrub that grows to twenty feet and has evergreen leaves and whitish to pink flowers. It thrives in the Carolinas but is equally good in Pennsylvania, Vermont, New Hampshire, and Maine.

Mountain rose-bay or Catawba Rhododendron (*R. catawbiense*) is a wild shrub of the eastern United States and has dark rose-lavender flowers in May and early June.

Some other native shrubs for woodlands are pieris, leucothoe, halesia, fothergilla, shadbush, witch hazel, wild roses, spiraea, holly grape, ceanothus, sourwood, dogwood, fringe tree, and crabapples. Berried plants include hollies, bayberry, viburnums, and snowberry. (See Chapter 7.)

Woodland Plants

Amelanchier canadense (serviceberry)
Arisaema triphyllum (Jack-in-the-pulpit)
Clethra alnifolia (sweet pepperbush)

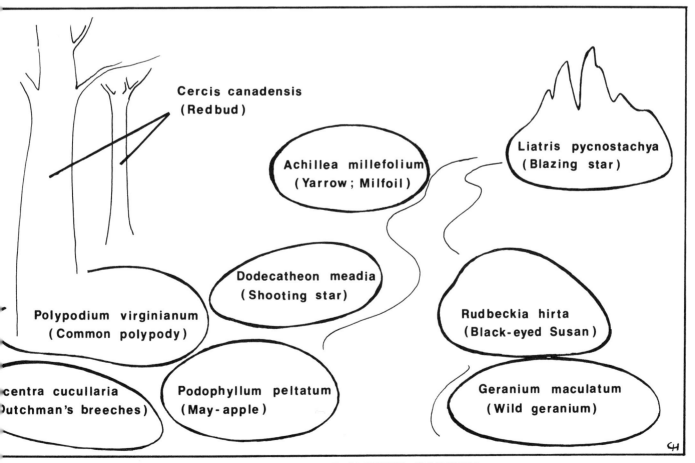

KEY TO MIDWEST NATIVE GARDEN

Cornus florida (flowering dogwood)
Cypripedium pubescens (yellow ladyslipper)
C. reginae (showy ladyslipper)
Geranium maculatum (wild geranium)
Lobelia cardinalis (cardinal flower)
Monarda didyma (bee-balm)
Myosotis (forget-me-not)
Podophyllum peltatum (May apple)
Symplocarous foetidus (skunk cabbage)
Trillium grandiflora (trillium)
Viburnum—many species

BOG GARDENS

Don't let the title of this section throw you; bog gardens can be unique additions to your property. Dramatic color is abundant here, and this landscape gives you the opportunity of getting acquainted with a fascinating group of plants.

Because the root runs for bog-garden plants must be cool, there has to be plenty of shade and dampness. We do not necessarily mean

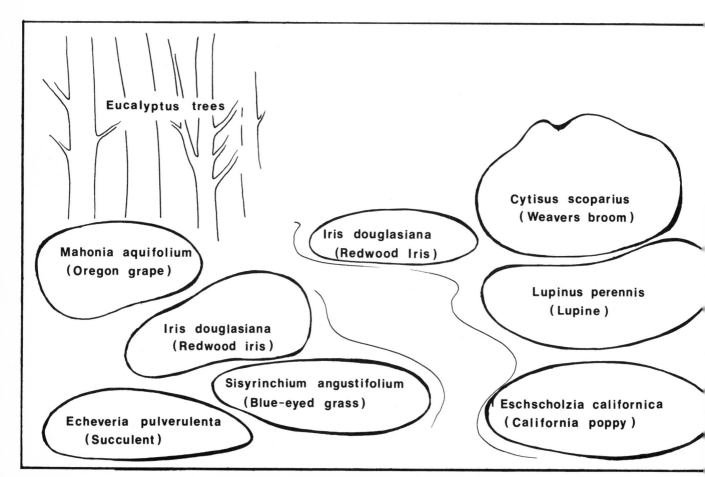

KEY TO WEST COAST NATIVE GARDEN

WEST COAST NATIVE GARDEN

a garden where stagnant water accumulates, although this is suitable habitat too. In my garden the situation is somewhat modified, with a hollow where soil stays constantly wet.

This garden should be located in a secluded nook or neglected cranny rather than close to the house (because of dampness). Neglected land can be turned into a veritable greenery with all kinds of unusual and appealing plants that will thrive in a bog garden. And best of all, once established, these gardens fend for themselves year after year without much attention from you.

Bog gardens are mysterious and dramatic; this fine example includes sweet flag and skunk cabbage, swamp maple and viburnum. (Photo by Molly Adams)

BOG GARDEN

BOG GARDEN PLANTS

Aconitum uncinatum (climbing aconite)
Asclepias incarnata (swamp milkweed)
Calopogon pulchellus (grass-pink orchid)
Caltha palustris (marsh marigold)
Gentiana andrewsi (closed gentian)
Houstonia caerulea (bluets)
Iris versicolor (iris)
Lobelia cardinalis (cardinal flower)
Pontederia cordata (pickerel weed)
Sagittaria latifolia (arrowhead)
Sarracenia purpurea (pitcher plant)
Symplocarpus foetidus (skunk cabbage)
Trillium—many species

For additional information on water plants, see the companion volume in this series: *Water Gardening*.

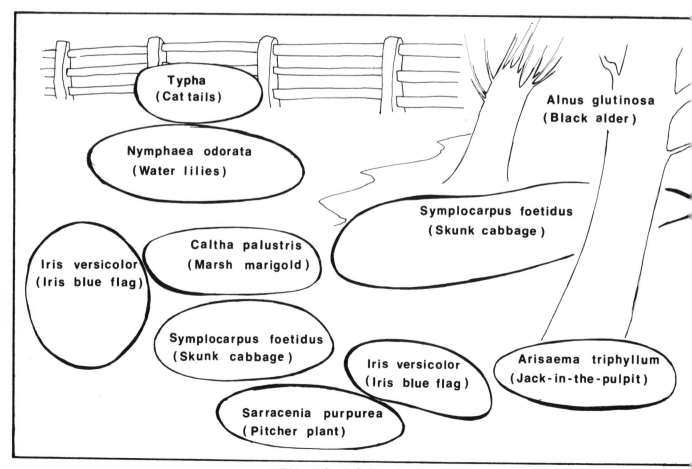

KEY TO BOG GARDEN

WILD FLOWERS IN THE CULTIVATED GARDEN

If you already have a garden and want to incorporate some wild flowers, by all means do so. Many will grow if selected properly and considered as spring-blooming perennials rather than as wild flowers. They become part of the total scene and add great beauty; furthermore, they look natural. Ideal wild flowers are violets, which you can add to many areas where there is some sun. The purple-blue *Viola cucullata* is impressive when mixed with yellow daffodils, and its foliage will hide the dying narcissus leaves when blooms fade. Wild white violets are an excellent choice for other areas where there is rich soil and some sun.

Dicentra exima, the wild bleeding heart, is a pretty plant that generally remains green all summer and blooms on and off through the season, adding sparkle to any flower bed. The black-eyed Susan (*Rudbeckia hirta*) is stellar for color and blooms on and off for many months; its orange color is a special accent. This plant, which revels in partial sun and rich moist soil, is generally a biennial and not at its best until the second year.

Goldenrod (solidago), which is popular in England, seems overlooked in this country, but it makes a dramatic splash of color even in a shaded area. In areas where nothing much will grow, the tall goldenrod will supply late summer color. *Solidago nemoralis* and *S. odora* are two good choices.

These (and other) native flowers will grow and bloom if you give them even moderate care; indeed, you may find them outperforming your regular garden plants. Use them in combination with your other flowers, but always plant them in groups and colonies so they act as a foil for the colors of other plants.

PLANTS FOR SUNNY SITES

Asclepia tuberosa (butterfly weed)
Aster novae-angliae (New England aster)
Callirhoe involucrata (poppy-mallow)
Helenium autumnale (sneezeweed)
Helianthus annuus (sunflower)
Heuchera sanguinea (coral bells)

Lupinus perennis (Eastern lupine)
Lythrum salicaria (purple loosestrife)
Monarda didyma (bee-balm)
Oenothera—many species
Phlox paniculata (summer phlox)
P. subulata (creeping phlox)
Potentilla fruticosa (cinquefoil)
Rudbeckia (black-eyed Susan)—(many species)
Solidago—many species
Thalictrum diocium (meadow rue)

This garden is natural in character and wildlings abound. The guest is immediately greeted by warmth and beauty. (Photo by Matthew Barr)

A shady woodland garden where many native plants thrive. This garden is easy to manage, looks natural, and is totally inviting. (Photo by Matthew Barr)

MY NATIVE GARDENS

My first native garden was in Northfield, Illinois, in the 1960s. On an acre of land was a 1930s-type house, with a great expanse of property in the rear. Bordering the grass area in a semi-circle was a natural forest preserve. Great oak trees towered above a wooded area deep with years of leaves. Time-worn, overgrown paths wandered through this wild wonderland filled with native species. I gardened this area extensively, carefully preserving the natural beauty. It became a showplace, and at one time I counted more than twenty-five native plants, including Jack-in-the-pulpit, May apple, many kinds of violets, three different types of trilliums, assorted ferns, and other plants. It was here I learned respect for the natives

This bog garden has ferns and grasses; note daffodils in background. (Photo by author)

In the author's side garden native hollyhocks are used against the fence; sun flowers are growing too. (Photo by author)

and how to care for them—it was an experience I would never trade for anything. I worked with what nature provided.

Unlike my Illinois home, my California home was new when I bought it. The site was barren except for the hill in the rear which had old oak and bay trees. Midway on the crest, under the trees, was a perfect spot for a woodland scene, so I planted ferns and rhododendrons interspersed with azaleas, ilex varieties and some euonymus. The bottom of the hill (which framed the house) was wet because of a nearby underground spring, so there I planted, in partial shade and sun, marsh marigolds, some native orchids, and other plants that like their feet wet.

In the spring I started on the south end of the property, which was very dry and very sunny. I planted a small grass area and bordered it with shrubs and ground cover appropriate for the locale. This garden soon flourished, although it needed copious watering during our dry summers. I mixed garden favorites such as gazanias and sweet Williams with native plants for a riot of summer color.

The east side of the house, which received intense sun, was protected by fencing, and had gravel-like soil. Here I installed a cactus and succulent garden with many plants native to Arizona and New Mexico: agaves, aloes, opuntias, and echinocactus. When winter came, I heavily mulched this hill with pebbles to keep the plant roots protected from cold. In two years I had only a few fatalities because the site was matched to the plants.

The conditions of the sunny, wild garden were a relatively rich (but not too rich) soil and moderate watering. Try to select a natural grassy place because these plants naturally grow side by side with grasses that act as a mulch and protect flower roots from scorching as they conserve moisture.

3. Getting Plants ✍

Where do you get native plants for your garden? Most people immediately think of collecting them in the woods, but there are other ways to have native plants: you can buy them from mail-order houses and you can also propagate your own—the latter method is much cheaper and certainly more fun.

Today there are many seed houses and plant suppliers that specialize in wild plants. They grow and propagate them, and these plants are generally more adaptable than plants from the forests. However, if you know of a wooded area where wild flowers abound and where the bulldozers are fast approaching, I see no reason why you shouldn't collect a few plants and save them from sure death. But first try to get permission from the land owners, and collect *only* what you can use. Don't rape the land; there are other people who love our wild plants too.

Plants have a better chance of surviving if you wait until they are dormant rather than blossoming. Collect spring-blooming plants in early fall and the fall-flowering types in spring. Before you dig up plants, make notes as to exactly what conditions they were growing in. Check the light situation and soil; you will have to try to duplicate these conditions to a good extent if you want your plants to survive the move.

Don't just rip a plant from the ground. Dig around it with a small spade, and take as much of the soil with it as you can to lessen the risk of root rot and shock to the plant. Once you have the plant, immediately wrap it in moist sphagnum moss (which you can carry with you), and put it into a plastic bag. Sprinkle it with water, and

31

Seeds of native plants can be started in flats, then provided with warmth and humidity for germination. (Photo by author)

keep the plant out of the sun; even a few minutes' exposure can kill the wildling. Put the plants in place in your garden immediately; don't let them stand for even a few hours because the quicker they are in the soil, the better their chance of survival. During the first few weeks, watch them for rot or mildew. Water them well, but don't flood them. If the transplant takes—some do, some don't—you have saved a piece of nature from the bulldozer.

SEEDS

If you know someone who has a wild-flower garden, ask if you can take some seed (few people will object). This is an excellent way of getting plants for your garden, and there is immense satisfaction in raising your own plants from seed. Also, seed-grown plants are generally stronger than collected or purchased specimens.

In addition to friends' flowers, there are always roadsides, secondary roads, and so forth where seed can be collected (this is best done about a month after flowering). Collecting may involve several trips to the site to be sure you get the seed, but it is well worth the effort because there is adventure here and endless fascination. When you are collecting seed, try to identify the plant from its basal leaves or from the flower if you have seen it bloom, although this isn't as easy as it sounds. I usually draw a rough sketch of the leaves and bloom and identify them later from books. (See Appendix.) To remove seed from the capsule or pods, crush lightly by hand or shake loose in a bag. Keep the seed in small, glass, corked bottles marked with the type of plant and date so you know what you have.

You can sow wild-flower seeds outdoors in most parts of the country after November 1; by then the temperature is cold enough to prevent immediate germination. In the spring, when the temperature reaches the desired warmth, from 45 to 65° F., germination will start. You can also mix the seed with some soil and store them in a Baggie in the refrigerator until spring and then sow outdoors. Still another method of working with wild-flower seeds is to start them in fall in container at least three inches deep. Use coffee cans, squatty

Here, seeds are started in peat pots. (Photo by author)

A seedling being put in individual pot for future growing. (Photo by author)

clay pots, etc. Planting mix can be vermiculite, perlite, or sand and peat. Keep the containers in a cool place, covered with plastic or glass. When seedlings are three to four inches high, transplant them to the open garden in spring.

No matter which of the above methods you use, once seeds are in the ground they need a good, rich, and porous soil, copious water (but not so much that mildew results), and good air circulation. One important suggestion: when seedlings are ready for the open ground, harden them off gradually, that is, expose them to outdoor weather a few hours a day for about a week before actually planting. I find this works extremely well rather than just immediately plunging plants into the ground because tiny seedlings cannot take a great shock.

OTHER PROPAGATION METHODS

Division, cuttings, and layering are other fine, quicker ways of increasing your plant supply. To divide a wild flower, dig down on the side of the plant, and cut the new plant off. (These new plants are sometimes called stolons, runners, or basal offshoots.) Any perennial that is a good-sized clump is fine for division. Dig the plant in early spring and sever it into chunks; each chunk has its own roots and thus becomes a new plant. You can also remove adventitious growths such as runners, stolons, or offshoots and pot these for new plants.

Layering is the best propagating method for shrubs and trees because it is simple and takes only a few minutes. In spring, notch out a small piece of wood from a branch that is near the ground. Treat the wound with root hormone powder, and then bury the branch (make sure the wound gets buried too) an inch or so, with the far tip of the branch exposed to the air. Put stone over the soil. Roots will grow at the point of the wound in a season or two (depend-

Cuttings can also be used for propagating plants; when roots show, they are potted individually. (USDA photo)

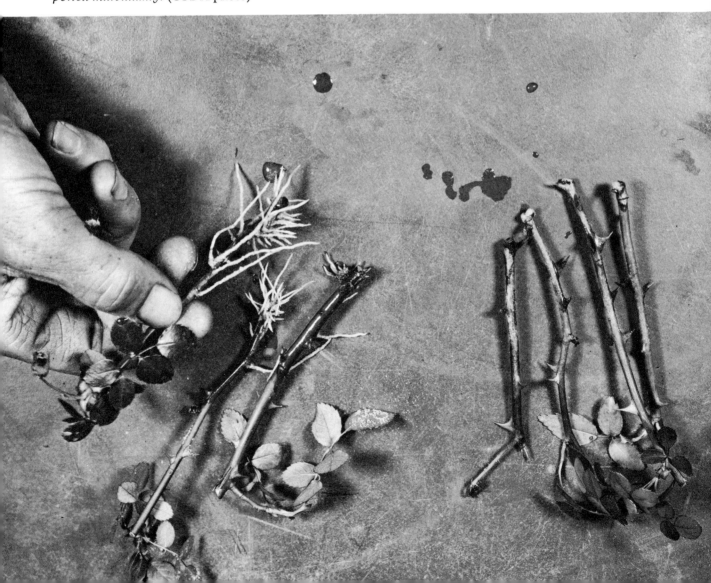

These cuttings are ready for planting. (USDA photo)

ing on the species), and you can then cut off the new plant from the mother plant.

An even simpler version of layering is air layering. Scrape a notch out of a branch that is about ten inches long. Treat the wound with hormone powder and then wrap a wad of moist sphagnum moss around it. Cover the moss with plastic, securing the plastic at both ends with string or waterproof tape. Leave the package alone for a season; in the second spring, unwrap the package to see if roots have formed. If they have, cut the new growth from the mother plant just below the newly rooted section and grow it on its own. If the layering has not taken, rewrap the package and wait another season.

Air layering is another method of plant propagation; a notch is made in branch and covered with sphagnum. (USDA photo)

Wrapped in plastic and tied at each end, this air layer will form roots. (USDA photo)

Crown division is a simple propagating method; merely separate crowns of plant and pot separately. (Photo by J. Barnich)

Hardwood cuttings is another propagation method. Cuttings are terminal shoots of a tree or shrub and are taken in late fall when growth is mature. Cut off a branch four- to six-inches long, and remove leaves on the bottom section. Dip the branch into root hormone powder, and insert it upright in equal parts of peat moss and sand (a clay flower pot is a satisfactory container). Cover the cutting with a plastic bag, and keep in a cool shaded spot over winter. By early spring, when new root shoots have started to form, bring the plant into more light, remove the plastic, and keep soil moderately moist. In another year the seedling will be ready for planting.

Softwood cuttings (taken in early summer) have rarely worked for me; rot is a constant enemy. The procedure is very similar to that used with hardwood cuttings.

4. Determining Factors: Temperature, Moisture, and Soil

Where you live generally dictates what kind of native plants you can grow successfully. Temperature, moisture, and soil all affect a plant's growth, and although there are ways to correct imbalance, basically the average gardener is better off accepting the conditions he has and choosing plants accordingly. For example, in the desert areas it is foolish to try to grow shady ferns, and a garden of tropical exotics in Illinois is doomed to death too. Fit the plant to the climate and site, or alter the site somewhat, and gardening will become a pleasure instead of a chore.

Soil

To start with native plants, test your soil; once you know whether it is acidic or alkaline you can proceed. (Soil test kits are available from suppliers.) Most woodland plants need an acid soil (5.5 to 6.0); other plants will respond in a neutral soil (7.0). After testing, prepare the soil—aerate and improve it. You must restore a clay soil's tilth so it is porous and crumbly. Dig down several feet; break up compacted soil, and add compost and peat moss. Use organic fertilizers to help break up a clay soil and to remedy sandy soils too; after you have conditioned the soil mix in some fresh top soil. If all this sounds like hard work, it is, but you will find that it is well worth the effort once the garden is in place and native plants become part of the property because they will thrive then and need only routine care.

For each group of plants mentioned in Chapter 2, prepare the appropriate soil. Remember, match and mate is the key to success.

Wet moist places favor Galax and ferns; the deep lush green leaves of Galax are crowned with white spires of flowers in summer. (Photo by Marjorie Dietz)

Native Plants for Different Situations

TREES—WET LOCATIONS
Abies balsamea (balsam fir)
Acer rubrum (red maple)
Betula nigra (black birch)
Carpinus caroliniana (American hornbeam)
Liquidambar styraciflua (sweet gum)
Quercus palustris (pin oak)
Thuja occidentalis (American arborvitae)
Tilia americana (American linden)
Tsuga canadensis (Northern Hemlock)

TREES—DRY LOCATIONS
Betula populifolia (gray birch)
Juniperus virginiana (red cedar)
Picea glauca (white spruce)
Pinus banksiana (Jack pine)
P. virginiana (scrub pine)
Quercus coccinea (scarlet oak)
Robinia pseudoacacia (black acacia)

Woodland garden natives are not all shade lovers; may-apple (CENTER) *and foam flower* (LOWER LEFT) *grow side by side with a native from China,* Rhododendron fortunei. (Photo by Marjorie Dietz)

SHRUBS—WET LOCATIONS
Clethra alnifolia (sweet pepperbush)
Euonymus americanus (strawberry bush)
Hamamelis virginiana (American witch-hazel)
Ilex glabra (inkberry)
I. verticillata (black alder)
Rhododendron nudiflorum (pinxter flower)
R. viscosum (white swamp honeysuckle)
Salix discolor (pussy willow)
Sambucus canadensis (American elder)
Vaccinium corymbosum (swamp blueberry)
Viburnum lentago (sheepberry)

SHRUBS—DRY LOCATIONS
Ceanothus americanus (New Jersey tea)
Elaeagnus commutato (silverberry)
Juniperus (various) (juniper)
Myrica pensylvanica (bayberry)
Potentilla fruticosa (cinquefoil)
Prunus maritima (beach plum)

For wild flowers and bulbs, see Chapter 5.

KNOW YOUR WEATHER

Knowing your weather is not as difficult as it sounds. Observe and take notes each year so you will know what kind of weather to expect in the four seasons. This will give you a clue as to what to plant and what not to plant in your locale. Follow the Hardiness Zone Map (see illustration) to help you determine plants for your site but do not use it as a rigid rule. Experiment. Be something of an adventurer. Many plants that should not grow in certain zones will tolerate somewhat lesser conditions of necessity, especially natives.

If you are just moving into an area, consult books or the local nursery and wild flower sanctuaries. Go hiking and observe native flora or ask neighbors what they grow in their garden.

Some plants need cooler conditions than you can give them; others, from warmer regions, may not be able to withstand the rigors of your

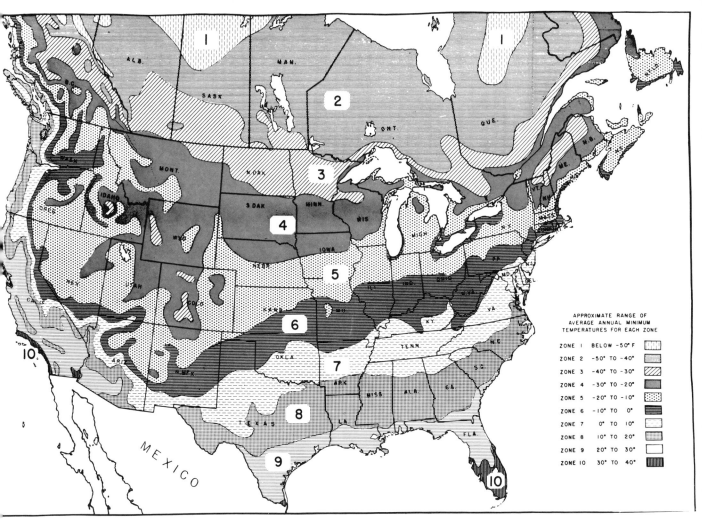

Plant Hardiness Zone Map. (USDA photo)

winters. In Illinois, my three attempts at rock gardening were miserable failures because summers were just too hot. And when I gardened in Florida many years ago, shade-loving plants that needed rich soils did not respond. Even within your own small plot there will be microclimates (little pockets) where the temperature is warmer or cooler than the mean average temperature of the property.

Hardiness

The Hardiness Zone Map of the United States is not as mysterious as some gardeners think. The map shows temperature ranges for plants in various parts of the country designated by Zone 1, Zone 2, and so forth. Locate your part of the country on the map so you have some idea of plant hardiness in your area. (Strictly speaking, you could just check temperatures with local bureaus to get similar information.) Note that the zones wiggle throughout the United States and that parts of Nevada, California, etc. are included in the same zone as southern Illinois, Indiana, Ohio, Pennsylvania, and so forth. Thus, you can be pretty sure then that anything that will grow in lower Illinois will also grow in parts of Ohio, Kentucky, and West Virginia too, other conditions being equal. However, remember that because there are many divergencies in zones (hills, lakes, and streams), plants from unrelated zones might prosper too. Therefore, although the map is immensely helpful, use it as a point of reference only, not as a dictum. California alone, which is classified as Zones 9 and 10, could be further divided into ten or twenty other zones!

Generally, Northern plants prefer cool weather and weak winter light—hot dry summers will kill them quickly. Altering your climate zone involves some work, but it can be done. For example, I grow many cacti and succulents from the dry zones of New Mexico and

This shady, city, woodland garden contains many native plants; Cimicifuga rhemosa *blooms at right.* (Photo by Pat Matsumoto)

These plants need a dry, hot, sunny site to prosper; in the open they make an impressive accent. (Photo by Molly Adams)

Arizona; I thoroughly mulch them in winter to protect them against freezing and thawing, and in summer I give them some shade.

In your own garden, as mentioned, there will be microclimates. Warm air rises, so the temperature will always be somewhat cooler at the bottom of a hill than at the top. Locations against the house wall will tend to be warmer than other areas on the same property since they are more protected (fences, barriers, etc.). Wind cools the temperature in summer, which is sometimes an advantage, but in winter, if there is little snow cover, a high wind can be incredibly drying. Remember to keep prevailing winds in mind when placing plants.

OPPOSITE: *In this photo, plants that like wet feet thrive near a pond.* (Photo by Ken Molino)

5.Wild Flowers ✍

Wild flowers are favorite native plants and many books have been written about them. Some cover specific states or sections of the country, others are more general. In any case, wild flowers are lovely harbingers of warm weather. There is no reason why these fine plants cannot be in our gardens so we can enjoy them regularly rather than occasionally.

For many years wild flowers held little interest for the average gardener. It has only been recently that our flowering gems have been "discovered" again. And today the wild flower garden is very possible to have because seed companies and suppliers now have plants to sell.

A true cultivated garden of wild flowers is hard to find and takes years to accomplish. In Michigan and Wisconsin I have encountered them and what a joy it is to see. For the most part I mix some wild flowers with my garden hybrids and thus have the best of two worlds.

Some wild flowers will need rich soil and moist conditions, while others will grow in almost any soil. It is difficult to simulate their native habitat. Ironically, once moved they seem to require varied conditions, and observation and experience is the key to success.

The problem is that there are so many wild flowers that it is difficult to say which ones are the best. Depending on where you live, the selection varies, but in very broad terms we might say that the following wild flowers are the most commonly grown and known and most adaptable to soil and climate over a wide area of the country:

Aquilegia canadensis (common American columbine). Red bells on 1-foot stems signal the arrival of columbine in your garden. There

48

Hepatica acutiloba *is a popular wild plant and does well in the garden where it needs a neutral soil.* (Photo by Pat Matsumoto)

are species for almost every state. Most plants need a rather dry, tight soil with half to full sun. Plants can be easily propagated by seed, and some may bloom the first year. Other species include *A. caerulea* (Colorado columbine), *A. chrysantha* (golden columbine), and *A. flavescens*.

Arisaema triphyllum (Jack-in-the-pulpit). This lovely forecaster of spring is robust and dependable, a good plant for the beginning gardener. Flower color differs with species, but generally is striped maroon to pale green with white lining. Arisaema prefers a rich woodsy soil in shade. Propagation is from offshoots in fall or from seed, which can be sown immediately.

Asarum canadense (wild ginger). An exceedingly good ground cover, lush and deep green and very easy to grow. Give plants a shady nook in moist soil, and propagate by division of rootstock at any time.

Claytonia virginica (spring beauty). In April, delicate pink flowers bloom in woodlands. *C. virginica* is native to the East, but there are also species for Western gardens. Plants need moist woodsy soil in shade. Progagate new plants from small tubers after leaves die. *C. caroliniana* (broadleaved spring beauty) is also lovely.

Dicentra cucullaria (Dutchman's breeches). Nodding flowers bear two spurs that make them look like pairs of white breeches hanging upside down. Grows mainly in Eastern woods, and foliage dies immediately after flowering. *D. eximia* and *D. formosa* are also good species. Plants like shade and a well-drained soil. Divide large clumps after flowering for new plants.

Dodecatheon meadia (shooting star). These are common plants in the Central and Western states; twenty species are widely distributed throughout these regions. They make excellent garden subjects. Petals point backward and make it seem as if the flower is shooting forward.

Hepatica triloba (americana) needs an acid soil; flowers are white or pink. (Photo by Pat Matsumoto)

In the West, red to white flowers are common. Plants need a partially shady location and neutral soil. Basal leaves disappear in summer. Divide dormant crowns for new plants.

Erythronium americanum (trout lily). In the Northeast, tiny yellow flowers appear in April. Dependable and easy to grow, trout lilies need deep moist soil and prefer shade, although they will tolerate sun. For new plants, take offshoots from mature ones. Seed sowing requires almost seven years for bloom.

Geranium maculatum (wild or wood geranium). These easy-to-grow plants are found in the East and North Central states, in a wide range of species. Pinky-lavender flowers above finely cut leaves are excellent April-May color. In large colonies, plants make a fine display. Geraniums like a humusy soil in partial shade. For new plants, divide old ones.

Hepatica americana (hepatica). In the East this is one of first wild flowers to appear in early spring. Flowers are pale blue or purple and are fine additions to a garden. *H. acutiloba*, with large flowers, is also desirable. Both species grow well in a somewhat gravely soil that is well drained. Divide clumps for new plants.

Iris cristata (crested iris). This fine iris can be grown in almost all states. It bears lovely crested blue flowers; spreads rapidly; is not choosy about soil; and is prized by many gardeners. In the Central states; *I. missouriensis* is popular. In the East, the blue flag *I. versicolor* is especially handsome. *I. verna* is also desirable. Some iris need dry hillside conditions, but others like rich and shady woodsy places. For new plants, divide rhizomes in spring.

Lobelia cardinalis (cardinal flower). Red flowers make this native especially worthwhile in the garden. Blooms in July to September. Plants like moist shady locations or full sun. Plants spread easily; for new ones, divide the fibrous roots of mature plants.

Mertensia virginica (Virginia bluebells). An easy and adaptable plant. Has clusters of porcelain blue bells on two-foot stems in April. After

WILD FLOWERS

Encelia farinosa
BOTTLE-BRUSH

Brodiaea pulchellum
COVENA

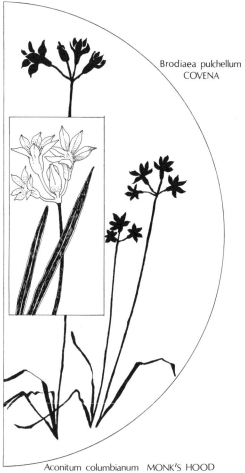

Anemone tuberosa TUBER ANEMONE

Aconitum columbianum MONK'S HOOD

flowering, plants die down completely. Provide a rather dry, lean soil and shade in summer for best results. Divide rootstocks after blooming for new plants, or sow seed.

Phlox divaricata (blue phlox). Some of our best garden flowers are found in this group. Several are low growers, with bristly foliage, and others are tall and stately. Most spread rapidly and are not bothered by pests or diseases. Blue phlox can be grown in twenty states; other species are suitable, depending on where you live. *P. stolonifera* has lavender flowers, and *P. drummondii*, an annual from Texas, has deep-red flowers. *P. longifolia*, and *P. subulata* (ground phlox), are other choice plants. Phlox need a woodsy soil in light shade. Get new plants by self-sowing seed or by division.

This colony of wild flowers in a garden spot is Penstemon nitidis, Phlox longifolia, *and* Lathyrus polymorphus. (Photo by Pat Matsumoto)

Sanguinaria canadensis (bloodroot). Bloodroot is an unfortunate name for a lovely plant that bears stellar white flowers with yellow stamens in late March, sometimes earlier. It likes a woodsy soil, and even though it appreciates spring sun, try to provide shade in summer. Obtain new plants from old ones by dividing the rootstock and planting one inch deep in fall. Or sow seed, press in, and cover with soil.

Solidago canadensis (goldenrod). Don't get this one mixed up with the plant that harbors hay fever: ragweed. Goldenrod is a fine plant for summer gardens; there are more than one hundred species. Plants need a sandy soil and revel in sun. Propagation is by division.

Trillium grandiflorum (large flowered trillium). These fine plants give a grand display; they are majestic in any garden, with large pink, red, purple, or white flowers. They are easy to grow, and there are trilliums for almost every state. In the East, *T. grandiflorum* is highly prized. *T. luteum*, from North Carolina, is yellow, and *T. erectum* is found in North and South Carolina; it has greenish-brown flowers. Other good trilliums include *T. cernuum*, with white flowers, and *T. sessile*, with red flowers. Grow the plants in shade with moist soil. To increase your trillium stock, divide rootstocks in fall and plant them four inches deep. Plants flower in the fourth or fifth year.

Viola (violets). There are seventy-five species throughout almost every state. Flowers range from yellow to violet to white to red-purple. Generally, violets prefer a moist shady spot, but they will also accept other conditions if necessary. Yellow species include *V. eriocarpa*, *V. pubescens*, and *V. rotundifolia*. Among the blue violets are *V. cucullata*, *V. pedata* (bird's-foot violet), *V. pedatifida*, and *V. sagittata*. Good white violets are *V. blanda* (sweet white violet), *V. canadensis*, and *V. primulifolia*.

MORE WILD FLOWERS

Achillea millefolium (yarrow). White flowers; easily grown favorite.

Aconitum columbianum (monk's hood). Helmet-shaped blue flowers.

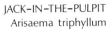

WILD FLOWERS

MARSH MARIGOLD
Caltha palustris

JACK-IN-THE-PULPIT
Arisaema triphyllum

YELLOW LADY'S SLIPPER
Cypripedium pubescens

BLOODROOT
Sanguinaria canadensis

Trillium erectum has brown or red flowers. It needs an acid soil and a cool moist place to thrive. (Photo by Pat Matsumoto)

Amsonia tabernaemontana (willow amsonia). Pale blue flowers in clusters. Sun.

Anemonella thalictroides (rue anemone). Flowers white or pink, about 1 inch across.

Aster erioconides (heath aster). Tiny white blooms. Sun.

A. linariifolius. Violet and yellow flowers. Sun.

Baptisia australis (wild blue indigo). Showy dark blue flowers. Sun.

Callirhoë involucrata (poppy mallow). Red-purple flowers; needs excellent drainage. Sun.

Caltha palustris (marsh marigold). Widespread range; lovely dark green foliage and bright yellow flowers.

Campanula divaricata. Tiny blue bells. Sun.

*C. americana** (star bellflower). Blue or white flowers.

C. rotundifolia (harebell). Violet blue bells on wiry stalks. Sun.

*Centaurea americana** (basket flower). Lavender or white flowers.

Cimicifuga racemosa. Small white flowers; lacy-like leaves. Shade.

Coreopsis lanceolata. Fine yellow flowers on wiry stems. Sun.

Cornus canadensis (bunchberry). Dainty white blossoms. Northern Maine.

Delphinium tricorne (wild larkspur). Deep blue flowers in East in early spring. Western species are *D. cardinale* (scarlet larkspur) and *D. nudicaule* (red larkspur), both with red flowers. Shade.

Dodecatheon radicatum (shooting star). Lovely rose or reddish flowers; Kansas to New Mexico range. Sun.

Echinacea (coneflower). Black-eyed susan's with white, pink, or purple rays. Sun.

Encelia farinosa (bottle-bush). California and Arizona native with bright yellow flowers. Sun.

Epilobium angustifolium (fireweed). Magenta flowers; long bloom period. Sun.

PENSTEMON   Penstemon heterophyllus

RED TRILLIUM   Trillium erectum

MAY-APPLE   Podophyllum peltatum

WILD FLOWERS

BROAD-LEAVED
SPRING BEAUTY
Claytonia caroliniana

FRINGED GENTIAN
Gentiana crinita

RUE ANEMONE
Anemonella thalictroides

SHOOTING STAR
Dodecatheon radicatum

*Eschscholzia californica** (California poppy). Golden orange flowers.

Gaillardia aristata (blanket flower). Bright yellow and red flowers. Mountains of the Northwest. Sun.

Galax aphylla. Heart-shaped leaves, white flowers in tall spikes. Shade.

Gelsemium rankinii (yellow jessamine). Delightful yellow flowers. Virginia to Florida, Alabama, and Texas.

*Gentiana crinita** (fringed gentian). Stunning, blue-fringed flowers. East.

*Gilia dianthoides** (ground pink). Lovely open-faced pink flowers. Southern California to Colorado.

Opuntia polyacantha *is low and spreading and bears yellow blooms.* (Photo by Pat Matsumoto)

Lilium superbum, turk's cap, is a popular wild plant for acid soil. Flowers are spotted orange (RIGHT). On the left is Allium giganteum, a ball of color. (Photo by Pat Matsumoto)

Helenium autumnale (sneezeweed). Yellow to red blooms. Sun.

Heuchera americana (alum root). Small greenish white or purple flowers in June. Shade.

Lupinus perennis (eastern lupine). Blue pea blossoms. Sun.

Lythrum salicaria (purple loosestrife). Tall stalks of airy purple flowers. Marshes and creeks of East Coast to Midwest.

Monarda didyma (bee-balm). Pink-lavender, red, or white types. Sun.

Nemophila menziesii (baby-blue eyes). Exquisite pale blue blooms. Coastal California.

Oenothera fruticosa (evening primrose). Bright yellow flowers. Sun.

Opuntia compressa (prickly pear). Showy, vivid, yellow blooms. Sun.

Penstemon heterophyllus (penstemon). Leaves spear-shaped; violet flowers. Sun.

Phacelia. Deep-blue flowers. Coastal California, Oregon, and Washington.

Physostegia virginiana (false dragonhead). Pink-lavender flowers. Sun.

Podophyllum peltatum (may-apple). Lovely white flowers and choice foliage. Shade. Eastern states.

Fritillarias and anemones are bulbous plants and give lovely color; there are many species, some natives and others from faraway countries. (Photo by Wayside Gardens)

Polemonium caeruleum (Jacob's ladder). Blue-violet bells and ferny foliage. Shade. Eastern states.

Polygonotum biflorum (Solomon's seal). Greenish pendant flowers on three-foot stems. Likes shade.

Rudbeckia (coneflower). Many species and colors. Extensively hybridized.

Ruellia ciliosa (wild petunia). Lavender-blue flowers. Sun.

Scutellaria serrata (showy skullcap). Violet-blue flowers. Sun.

Shortia galacifolia (Oconee bells). Lovely white flowers; need shade.

Silene virginica (fire pink). Vivid red flowers. Sun. *S. caroliniana* (wild pine), also desirable.

Sisyrinchium angustifolium (blue-eyed grass). Grassy leaves; small blue flowers.

Stokesia laevis (Stoke's aster). Pale blue to lavender flowers. Sun.

Talinum teretifolium (sunbright). Rosy pink blooms with yellow stamens.

Thalictrum dioicum (early meadow-rue). Panicles of fluffy purple stamens. Shade.

* Annuals

Bulbs

Most of us are familiar with bulbs. We know the tulips and daffodils or the big flowered begonias or dainty crocus. The bulbous plants are easy to grow for within the confines of the bulb are the makings of the new plant. All we do is plant and water. When we speak of bulbs here we also include rhizomes, corms, tubers—plants that have a thickened storage stem under the ground.

Our native bulbs are not well known and they deserve more attention. Alliums for one, I believe are extremely rewarding plants with lovely flowers. Brodiaeas from the West Coast are beauties too. *Convallaria majalis* (lily-of-the-valley) is better known; its scent having made it popular.

In the garden native bulbs can add great charm and color for little effort. Tuck them into nooks and crannies for delightful surprises. Many gardeners have rarely seen Calochortus or Camassia bloom, so they are in for lovely surprises. Like most bulbs, the natives need a good rich soil and excellent drainage. While you might find some of them growing in bog situations in the wild, in your garden they will still need a location that offers good drainage.

After plants have bloomed, allow the foliage to ripen naturally. *This is important* so that they can produce nutrients in the bulb for another year's flowering. Water and allow the leaves to grow as long as possible.

Allium (wild onion). Lovely flowers and so easy to grow. *A. stellatum* has pinkish flowers and *A. cernum* bears white on pink blooms. *A. serratum* is California native.

Brodiaea. West Coast bulbous plants that can be tried in the East. Flowers range from pure white to yellow to purple and blue. Provide a well-drained gravely soil in a hot sunny place. *B. pulchellum* has purple flowers.

Calochortus (mariposa lily). An overlooked fine plant with splendid flowers. Colors range from white to yellow or purple to blue. Plant in gravely, well-drained soil, and mulch in winter to protect against alternate freeze and thaw. Seeds available from West Coast suppliers.

Camassia (Indian lily). An ideal native bulbous plant quite amenable in most situations. May-blooming flowers vary from pure white and pale blue to dark purple. Provide rich moist soil for camassias. When leaves die in summer, reduce moisture. Generally available.

Clintonia (yellow blood lily). This beauty needs coolness and a shady spot. The tiny yellow flowers are charming in May and June. Species to try are the yellow *C. borealis*, the white *C. umbellata*, or the red *C. andrewsiana*.

Convallaria majalis (lily-of-the-valley). Well-known leafy green plant with fragrant white flowers. Needs rich soil and a shady spot. Eventually forms large clumps.

Fritillaria. Many of these; some small and others tall. *F. biflora* with brownish flowers and *F. purrdyi*, pink, need sun. In shade try *F. lanceolata*, a dark purple, or *F. atropurpurea*, purple.

Lewisia rediviva (bitter root). Rose or white flowers. Very handsome blooms and delights in any garden. They need a gravely sharp, drained soil with sun. Try these; they are stellar—*L. tweedyi* is most popular species.

Liatris pycnostachys (blazing star). Rose-purple or white flowers. Easy to grow in almost any type of soil. Keep in a sunny site.

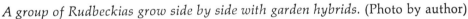

A group of Rudbeckias grow side by side with garden hybrids. (Photo by author)

Lilium (lily). Mainly white, orange, or orange-red flowers. *L. superbum*, (turk's cap) is most frequently grown. Spotted orange flowers make it desirable. Needs acid soil.

Smilacina (false Solomon's seal). Rhizomatous plants with small white or greenish flowers. They need a slightly acid soil. Use in moist shady places. *S. sessifolia*, Western favorite.

Zephyanthes (zephyr-lily). Handsome group of bulbous plants with bright green foilage and funnel form lovely flowers—white, yellow, pink. *S. atamasco*, generally grown. Need winter protection.

6. Trees ✐

Trees should be part of any attractive landscape plan. The versatile American trees can be used for shade, as lovely spring flowers, autumn color, and beauty. When selecting trees, pay attention to form: weeping, columnar, canopy, or branching; each has its place in the garden.

Because trees are the structure of your garden, get them growing as soon as possible. Most transplant best when they are young, and within a few years they will be thriving. Replanting trees because of poor placement requires time and energy and should be avoided, so decide where you want the tree, dig large holes, and use the *best* soil to get them growing.

Select trees with a specific purpose in mind. Do you need shade or a windbreak? Do you want spring color, or is autumn decoration more important? Are you going to use evergreens that are handsome all year?

There are many native trees, which can serve many purposes; the following list suggests some of the best (and includes hardiness tolerance):

*Abies balsamea** (balsam fir). Needlelike leaves to 1 inch, horizontal branches, and purple, oblong cones to 2½ inches long. −35 to −20° F.

*A. concolor** (white fir). Grows to 120 feet. Stiffly pyramidal and narrow, with horizontal branches and needlelike leaves to 2 inches long. −20 to −10° F.

Acer rubrum (red maple). Grows to 120 feet. Round head when mature. Dense foliage, with three to five lobes on 4-inch leaves. Leaves turn bright red in autumn. −35 to −20° F.

A. saccharum (sugar maple.) Grows to 120 feet. Round head when mature. Dense foliage; leaves are lobed to 6 inches across and turn yellow or orange and red in autumn. −35 to −20° F.

Aesculus glabra (Ohio buckeye). Grows to 30 feet. Rounded head. Coarse foliage, with five leaflets. Small, greenish-yellow panicles 6 inches high in mid-May; turn brilliant orange in autumn. −35 to −20° F.

Amelanchier canadensis (serviceberry). Grows to 60 feet. Open foliage (grayish when young) that is upright and often narrow with small, white, nodding racemes in late April. Yellow to red berrylike fruit in autumn, turning maroon-purple in early summer. −20 to −10° F.

A. grandiflora (apple serviceberry). Grows to 25 feet. Dense foliage with wide spreading branches. Flowers, tinged with pink when first open and pure white in early May, are 1¼ inches in diameter. Red to black edible berries in early summer. −20 to −10° F.

Betula papyrifera (white birch). Grows to 100 feet. Open foliage, with ovate leaves to 4 inches long. Cones are cylindrical, to 2 inches long. White bark peels off in paper-thin sheets. Yellow in autumn. −50 to −35° F.

Carya glabra (pignut). Grows to 40 feet. Slow-growing tree. Usually five serrated leaflets. Close but not shaggy bark. −20 to −10° F.

C. ovata (shagbark hickory). Grows to 120 feet. Compound leaves to 6 inches long with five to seven leaflets. Narrow and upright, with bark flaking off in loose plates. Golden brown in autumn. −20 to −10° F.

Cercis canadensis (eastern redbud). Grows to 40 feet. Flat top, irregular shape. Roundish, abruptly acute leaves. Pealike flowers in

The shadblow tree, Amelanchier arborea, *is a medium-sized tree that prefers a shady moist place.* (Photo by Molly Adams)

clusters, rosy-pink in color, and about ½ inch long. Open foliage that turns yellow in autumn. −20 to −10° F.

*Chamaecyparis lawsoniana** (Lawson false cypress). Grows to 120 feet. Slender to broadly pyramidal in shape, with evergreen, scale-like foliage. Branches are usually drooping, and the branchlets are frondlike. Has shredding bark. −10 to −5° F.

Chionanthus virginica (fringetree). Grows to 30 feet. Oblong leaves to 8 inches long and panicles to 8 inches in length. White and feathery in May-June, dark blue grapelike clusters of fruit in fall, and bright yellow in autumn. A deciduous tree. −20 to −10° F.

Pinus taeda, *known as the loblolly pine, grows large but is quite handsome in* *stature.* (USDA photo)

Cladrastis lutea (yellowwood). Grows to 50 feet. Rounded, dense foliage; leaves have seven to nine ovate leaflets. Pendulous clusters of fragrant white flowers that turn orange to yellow in autumn. -35 to $-20°$ F.

Cornus florida (flowering dogwood). Grows to 40 feet. Definite horizontal branching. Dense, lustrous foliage; ovate leaves to 6 inches long. Flowers are in dense heads, subtended by four large white petal-like bracts. True flowers in mid-May; inconspicuous bright red berries in tight clusters in fall. Scarlet in autumn. -20 to $-10°$ F.

Crataegus nitida (glossy hawthorn). Grows to 30 feet. Round headed. Thorny and dense branching. Coarsely toothed, lustrous leaves. White flowers in late May. Dull red fruit, ⅜ inch in diameter, ½ inch long, all winter. Orange to red in autumn. -20 to $-10°$ F.

C. phaenopyrum (Washington thorn). Grows to 30 feet. Broadly columnar, with round head. Thorny and dense branching. Lustrous and dense leaves have three to five lobes. White flowers ½ inch in diameter in many clusters in mid-June. Bright red fruit, ¼ inch in diameter, in winter. Scarlet to orange in autumn. -20 to $-10°$ F.

C. viridis (green hawthorn). Grows to 40 feet. Rounded and thorny. Spreading, dense, branching and dense foliage, with oblong, ovate, or elliptic-lanceolate leaves to 2½ inches long. White flowers ¾ inch in diameter borne in flat clusters 2 inches across in late May. Bright red fruit, ¼ inch in diameter in fall and winter. -20 to $-10°$ F.

Diospyros virginiana (common persimmon). Grows to 75 feet. Round headed. Often has pendulous branches. Bark deeply cut into small blocks. Dense foliage with ovate leaves to 6 inches long. Yellow to orange fruit 1½ inch in diameter, edible after frost. Yellow in autumn. -20 to $-10°$ F.

Fagus grandifolia (American beech). Grows to 90 feet. Densely pyramidal. Dense foliage, with ovate or oblong leaves to 5 inches long. Leaves are dark bluish-green above. Light gray bark. Golden bronze in autumn. -35 to $-20°$ F.

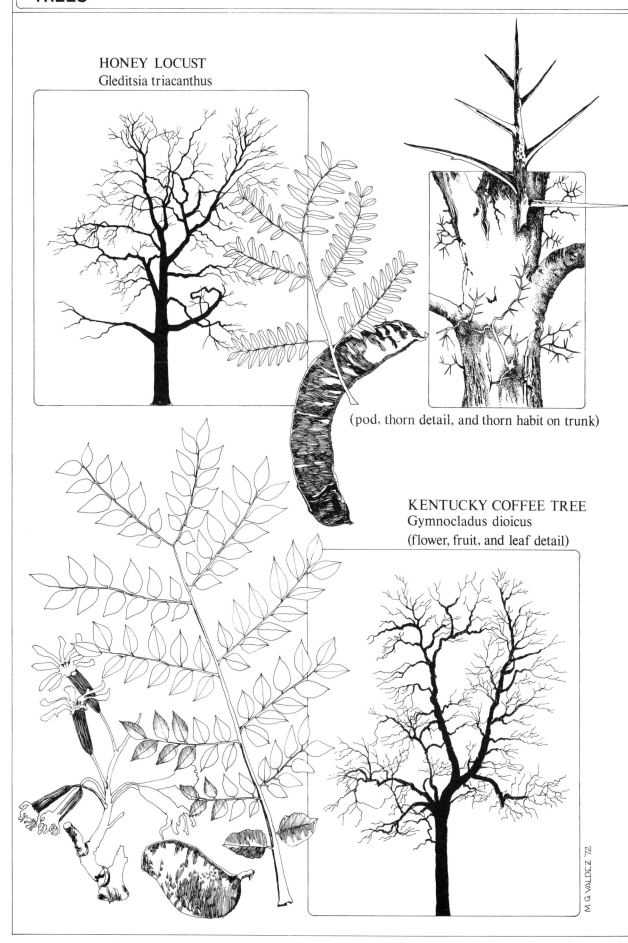

HONEY LOCUST
Gleditsia triacanthus

(pod, thorn detail, and thorn habit on trunk)

KENTUCKY COFFEE TREE
Gymnocladus dioicus
(flower, fruit, and leaf detail)

M. G. VALDEZ '72

Franklinia alatamaha (franklinia). Grows to 30 feet. Upright. Loose and open foliage, with leaves to 6 inches long. Brilliant orange to red in autumn. −10 to −5° F.

Fraxinus pennsylvanica (red ash). Grows to 60 feet. Dense and rounded tree with lovely yellow autumn color. Vigorous, good. −50 to −35° F.

Gleditsia triacanthus (honey locust). Grows to 140 feet. Broad, open, and fine textured foliage, with single and double compound leaves 7 to 12 inches long. −20 to −10° F.

Gymnocladus dioicus (Kentucky coffee tree). A good winter tree with picturesque branching habit. Seldom seen, but robust. −20 to −10° F.

Halesia carolina (carolina silverbell). Grows to 40 feet. Pyramidal to round topped. Coarse, open foliage, with oval or ovate leaves to 5 inches long. White bell-shaped flowers ¾ inch long in mid-May. Dry, three- to four-winged pod fruit, 2 inches long in fall. Yellow in autumn. − 10 to −5° F.

H. monticola (mountain silverbell). Grows to 100 feet. Pyramidal to round topped. Coarse, open foliage, with oval or oblong leaves to 11 inches in length. White bell-shaped flowers to 1 inch long in mid-May. Two-inch long fruit on a two- to four-winged pod. Yellow in autumn. −10 to −5° F.

*Ilex opaca** (American Holly). Grows to 50 feet. Pyramidal. Dense branching. Evergreen foliage, with spiny, and dense unlustrous leaves. Smooth light gray bark. Bright red berries ¼ inch in diameter on female plants of current year's growth in fall and early winter. −10 to −5° F.

*Juniperus virginiana** (red cedar). Grows to 100 feet. Densely pyramidal and often columnar. Evergreen, scalelike; foliage varies greatly. Bark shreds in long strips. Female plants have berries ¼ inch in diameter, ripening the first season in fall and winter. −50 to −35° F.

NATIVE TREES

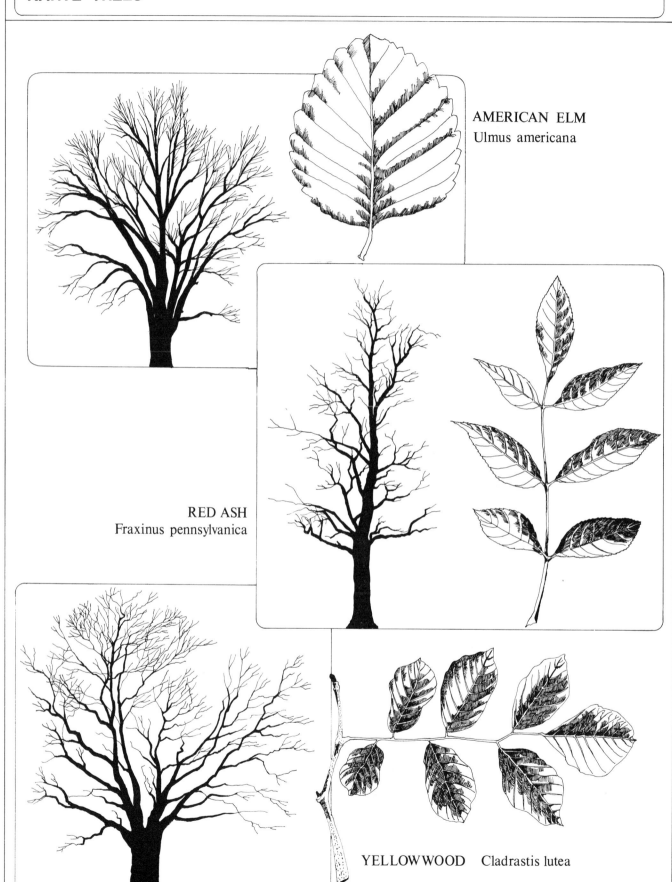

AMERICAN ELM
Ulmus americana

RED ASH
Fraxinus pennsylvanica

YELLOWWOOD   Cladrastis lutea

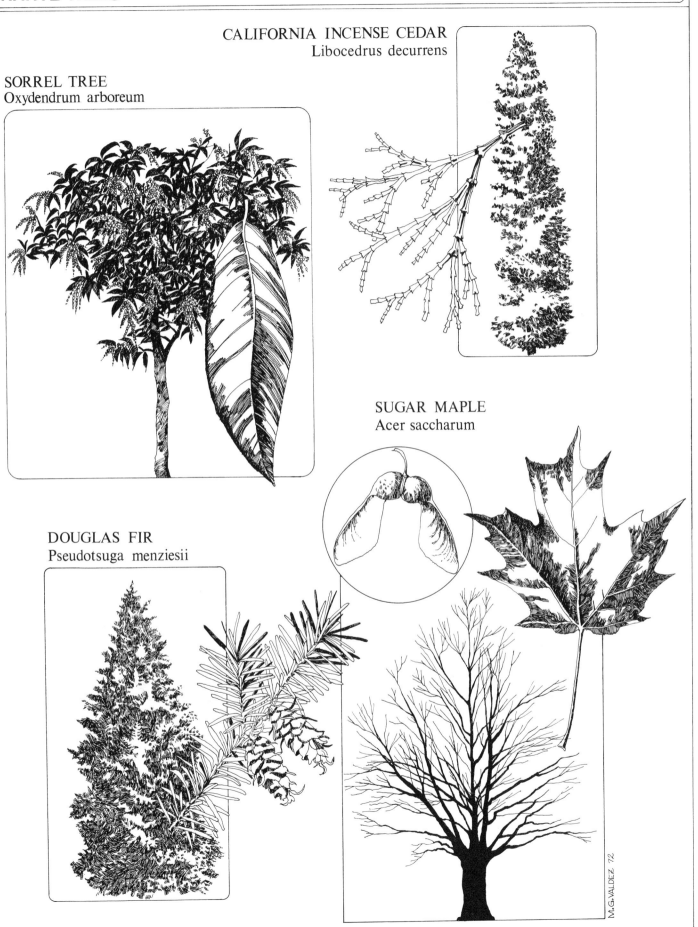

CALIFORNIA INCENSE CEDAR
Libocedrus decurrens

SORREL TREE
Oxydendrum arboreum

SUGAR MAPLE
Acer saccharum

DOUGLAS FIR
Pseudotsuga menziesii

M.G. VALDEZ 72

NATIVE TREES

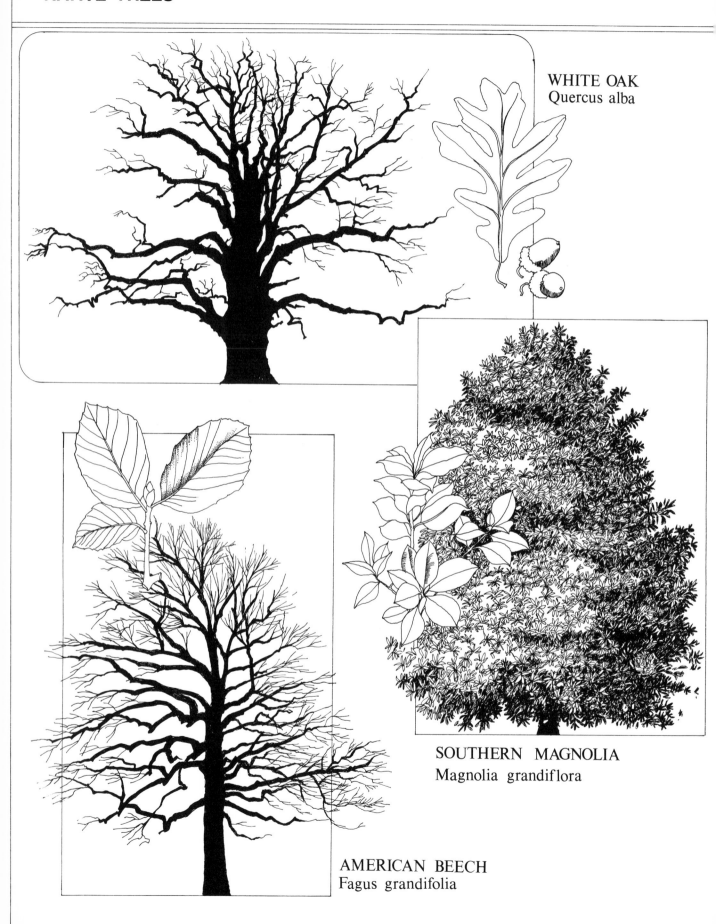

WHITE OAK
Quercus alba

SOUTHERN MAGNOLIA
Magnolia grandiflora

AMERICAN BEECH
Fagus grandifolia

*Libocedrus decurrens** (California incense cedar). Grows over 100 feet. Fine columnar habit; evergreen, scalelike leaves. Good ornamental tree. −10 to −5° F.

Liquidambar styraciflua (sweetgum). Grows to 140 feet. Broadly pyramidal and star shaped. Dense foliage, with leaves of five to seven lobes. Branches often have corky twigs. Deeply furrowed bark. Fruit and round horned balls 1 inch in diameter in fall. Scarlet in autumn. −10 to −5° F.

Liriodendron tulipifera (tulip tree). Grows to 200 feet. Broadly pyramidal. Massive branches. Eventually has a columnar, unbranched trunk. Dense foliage with square-shaped leaves. Greenish-yellow flowers marked with orange, tulip-shaped, in mid-June. Dry pods 2 to 3 inches long. Yellow in autumn. −20 to −10° F.

Magnolia acuminata (cucumber tree). Grows to 100 feet. Pyramidal and upright while young; massive, with wide-reaching branches at maturity. Dense leaves 5 to 10 inches long. The rather inconspicuous flowers are greenish-yellow and 3 inches high in early June, fruit pink to red in peculiar cucumber-shaped shells in early fall. −20 to −10° F.

M. grandiflora (Southern magnolia). Grows to 100 feet. Pyramidal. Usually dense and evergreen. Leaves 5 to 8 inches long and dropping at end of second year. White, fragrant flowers 8 inches in diameter, with usually six petals in late May; peculiar cucumberlike pods split open to disclose red seeds in early fall. −5 to −10° F.

M. macrophylla (large-leaved cucumber tree). Grows to 50 feet. Round-headed and open. Leaves are often 20 to 30 inches long and 10 inches wide and very coarse. Fragrant, creamy white flowers are 10 to 12 inches in diameter with six petals in early July. Fruit in peculiar cucumberlike pods split open to reveal red seeds in early fall. −10 to −5° F.

M. virginiana (sweet bay). Grows to 60 feet. Tree in the South; shrub in the North. Half evergreen in the South, green above and white

EASTERN REDBUD
Cercis canadensis (fruit pod, leaf, and branch with flowers)

PIGNUT
Carya glabra

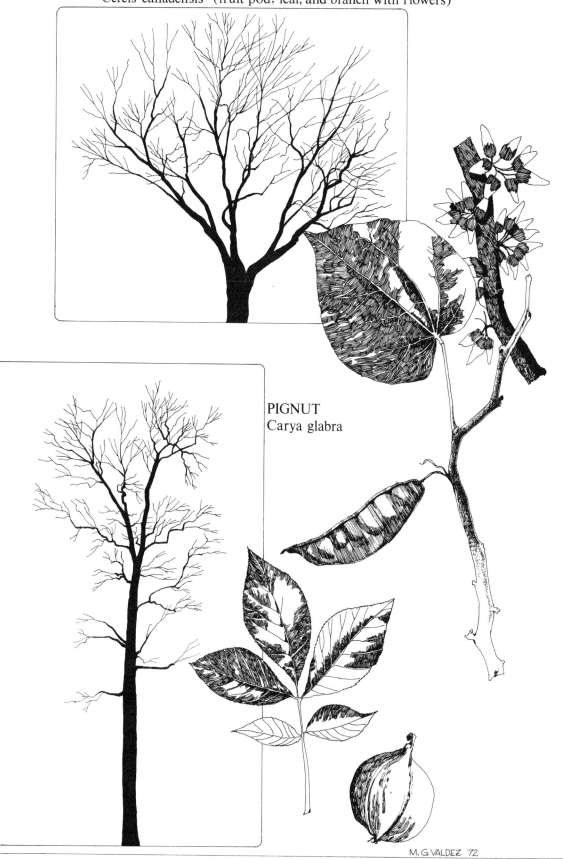

M. G. VALDEZ '72

below. Oblong leaves are 2½ to 4½ inches long. Fragrant white flowers with leaves 2 to 3 inches in diameter in June. Cucumber pods split open in early fall to disclose red seeds. −10 to −5° F.

Oxydendrum arboreum (sorrel tree). Grows to 75 feet. Pyramidal. Lustrous, dense, and leathery foliage. Small white flowers in slightly pendulous racemes in mid-July. Fruit in dried capsules far into the winter. Brilliant scarlet in autumn. −20 to −10° F.

*Picea glauca** (white spruce). Grows to 90 feet. Pyramidal evergreen with light bluish-green needles. −50 to −35° F.

*P. g. conica** (dwarf white spruce). Grows to 10 feet. Pyramidal and compact evergreen, with needles light bluish-green. −35 to −20° F.

The beauty of our native trees is well displayed in these white birches, Betula papyrifera. (USDA photo)

Pinus ponderosa* (Western yellow pine). Grows to 150 feet. Upright, open, and evergreen with, two or three needles 5 to 11 inches long in a bundle. Ovoid-oblong cones are to 6 inches long. −10 to −5° F.

P. strobus* (white pine). Grows to 150 feet. Rounded or pyramidal. Evergreen with five soft and flexible needles 2½ to 5½ inches long in a bundle. Cylindric cones are to 4 inches long. −35 to −20° F.

Prunus americana (American plum). Grows to 30 feet. Ovate, dull, and sharply serrated leaves. Flowers are about 1 inch across with calyx-lobes (not glandular). Fruit, which is about ¾ inch in diameter but in some strains larger, is yellow or red. −35 to −20° F.

Pseudotsuga menziesii* (Douglas fir). Grows to 300 feet. Pyramidal. Branching and horizontal evergreen, with needlelike and dense foliage. Fruit and pendulous cones 2 to 4½ inches long in fall and winter. −10 to −5° F.

Quercus alba (white oak). Grows to 100 feet. Broad round head. Wide spreading branches. Dense foliage that is purplish-red to violet purple in autumn. Deciduous, ovate leaves to 9 inches long, with five to nine entirely obtuse lobes. −20 to −10° F.

Q. coccinea (scarlet oak). Grows to 80 feet. Open and round-topped head. Rather lustrous but open foilage that is brilliant scarlet in autumn. Bright green deciduous, oblong, or elliptic leaves to 6 inches in length, seven to nine very deep lobes. −20 to −10° F.

Robinia pseudoacacia (black acacia). Grows to 80 feet. Upright. Few branches. Open foilage with seven to nine oval leaflets. Fragrant white flowers in pendulous clusters in May-June. Reddish-brown, pods to 4 inches long. −35 to −20° F.

Salix nigra (black willow). Grows to 35 feet. Lance-shaped leaves to 5 inches long, pale green underneath. −20 to −10° F.

Sorbus americana (American mountain ash). Grows to 30 feet. Leaves have eleven to seventeen leaflets and are to 4 inches long. Flowers are about 1/5 inch across. −50 to −35° F.

Poplar, dogwood, and cedar trees are an asset to any garden. (Photo by Molly Adams)

Stewartia ovata (mountain stewartia). Grows to 15 feet. Shrub. Flowers are to 3 inches across, with white stamens and orange anthers. −10 to −5° F.

Taxus brevifolia* (western yew). Grows to 45 feet. Dark yellowish-green leaves are 1 inch or less in length and are abruptly pointed. Fruit in August-September. −50 to −35° F.

T. canadensis* (ground hemlock). Grows to 6 feet. Dark yellowish-green, sharply pointed leaves are 1 inch long. Fruit in August. −50 to −35° F.

*Thuja occidentalis** (American arborvitae). Grows to 60 feet. Almost columnar. Evergreen with scalelike and flat foliage. Glandular leaves are yellowish-green beneath. Cones are ½ inch long. −50 to −35° F.

Tilia americana (American linden). Grows to 120 feet. Narrowly pyramidal. Broad-ovate leaves to 6 inches or more in length. Leaves are acuminate, with long-pointed teeth and glabrous beneath. Turn yellow in autumn. −50 to −35° F.

*Tsuga canadensis** (Northern hemlock). Grows to 90 feet. Long, slender, and horizontal to sometimes drooping branches from a pyramidal head. Evergreen, dense, needlelike foliage. Stalked cones are to ¾ inch long. −35 to −20° F.

*T. caroliniana** (Southern hemlock). Grows to 75 feet. Compact, pyramidal. Often with somewhat pendulous branches. Evergreen, needlelike, and dense foliage. Leaves entire, obtuse, or slightly notched at apex, glossy dark green above. Cones to 1½ inch long. −30 to −10° F.

Ulmus americana (American elm). Grows to 100 feet. Vase-shaped with arching branches. Leaves lobed and toothed. −50 to −35° F.

* Evergreen

7. Shrubs ✐

Shrubs, unfortunately, are generally taken for granted, and most gardeners do not know too much about them. Yet, when strategically placed, shrubs are ideal in most gardens and so deserve more attention. Suitable shrubs and care can make your garden a showplace, because once planted, shrubs are part of the landscape for many years.

Our native shrubs are better than the sophisticated hybrids because they are generally more robust, can withstand disease, and are suited to our climates. Proper selection is, of course, the key to success. Our American shrubs can, with proper selection, provide year-round color, and although perennials and annuals are lovely, shrubs are the framework of the garden.

In a new garden, placement of shrubs may be difficult until you are familiar with the sun orientation. Adding new shrubs to established plantings, however, is simple, and picking sun and shade areas can be done easily. And do plant according to the shrub's needs: some require sun, but others need shade.

Allow three to five feet between bushes so they have growing room, or you will soon have a jungle. Remember that most shrubs don't need or want excessive pruning and cutting. Allow them to grow naturally and they will become handsome specimens.

When you plant shrubs, dig deep holes; for a shrub two feet high, dig at least two feet and at least twice the diameter of the shrub's burlapped bag. Use the best soil you can afford. Cut the burlap when you insert the shrub in the hole, and arrange roots so they will grow outward (if they grow inward they strangle themselves). When the

83

NATIVE SHRUBS

SHRUBBY CINQUEFOIL
Potentilla fruticosa

COMMON WITCH-HAZEL
Hamamelis virginiana

CATAWBA RHODODENDRON
Rhododendron catawbiense

ARROWWOOD VIBURNUM
Viburnum dentatum

MOUNTAIN LAUREL   Kalmia latifolia

SNOWBERRY   Symphoricarpos albus

AMERICAN CRANBERRY BUSH
Viburnum trilobum

HOBBLE BUSH
Viburnum lantana

hole is half filled, run in water, soak the soil, and then fill the hole with soil. Leave a depression around the plant an inch or so lower than the surrounding soil.

Now thoroughly moisten the soil again, and throughout the first few weeks continue liberal waterings and give the plant more attention than usual, until it is established. Do not feed the first season until root systems are growing well; after that, apply weak fertilizers according to the directions on the package.

Your choice of shrubs will depend on many variables: climate; whether you want spring color or autumn leaves or whether you need spreading shrubs or tall ones; and finally, how the shrubs fit into the total plan of the garden. You don't want too many shrubs, but you do need enough to create a good framework for your native garden. The following notes will give you many helpful hints and information for when you select shrubs.

Azaleas, from the rhododendron family, are still listed in catalogs as azaleas, so we shall classify them that way too. Generally, these members of the heath family need an acid soil, and although hybrid azaleas for sunny exposures have been recently made available, the natives definitely need a shady spot. If your soil is not acid, but you still want azaleas, oak leaves and fir bark will help to correct the soil somewhat, but you will really have to dig down (at least two feet) and replace the existing soil.

Quite frankly, I prefer azaleas under trees; by themselves they look too leggy and dainty, but with trees as companions *they seem perfectly suited to a locale.* Flower color among the natives varies from white to shades of pink and rose; flowers are somewhat smaller than those of hybrids. Here are some good azaleas to try:

Azalea (Rhododendron) arborescens (sweet azalea). Grows to 10 feet. Bright green foliage that turns dark glossy red in autumn. Leaves to 3 inches long. White, very fragrant flowers in mid-June. −20 to −10° F.

OPPOSITE: *Native shrubs bank this small city garden and make fine background for native Liatrus.* (Photo by Pat Matsumoto)

NATIVE SHRUBS

NORTHERN BAYBERRY   Myrica caroliniensis

BUTTONBALL BUSH   Cephalanthus occidentalis

PINK SUMMERSWEET CLETHRA   Clethra alnifolia

RED OSIER   Cornus stolonifera

A. R. calendulaceum (flame azalea). Grows to 10, rarely 15 feet. Deciduous. Leaves to 3 inches long, pubescent when young. Orange-yellow to scarlet, funnel-shaped flowers 2 inches across in May-June. −20 to −10° F.

A. R. canadense (rhodora). Grows to 3 feet. Dull bluish-green foliage. Leaves are about 2 inches long. Rose-purple, two-lipped flowers to ¾ inch long in mid-May. −50 to −35° F.

A. R. catawbiense (catawba rhododendron). Great clusters of rose-purple flowers and shiny green leaves. Magnificent native and well-liked. Grows well in partial shade and moist soil. −20 to −10° F.

A. R. macrophyllum. Handsome Western native that grows to 10 feet; pink or almost purple flowers. −20 to −10° F.

A. R. maximum. Spreading shrub that grows to 10 feet. Pale rose flowers in July (which is rather late for rhododendrons). − 30 to −20° F.

A. R. nudiflorum (pinxter flower). Grows to 6 feet. Deciduous; Leaves to 3 inches long, glabrous and green underneath or hairy on the midrib. Flowers, pink to nearly white, are funnel shaped, 1½ inches across, and bloom April to May. −35 to −20° F.

A. R. occidentale (western azalea). Grows to 10 feet. Deciduous. Leaves to 4 inches long. White or pinkish flowers, with a yellow blotch, 1½ to 2 inches in diameter in late May. Scarlet and yellow in autumn. −10 to −5° F.

A. R. roseum (rosehall azalea). Grows to 9 feet. Dull bluish-green foliage. Fragrant bright pink flowers are 2 inches in diameter and bloom in late May. At one time considered a form of *R. nudiflorum.* −35 to −20° F.

A. R. vaseyi (pinkshell azalea). Grows to 15 feet. Deciduous. Five-inch leaves. Rose spotted with brown, two-lipped flowers are 1½ inches across and bloom in mid-May. Light red in autumn. −20 to −10° F.

A. R. viscosum (white swamp honeysuckle). Grows to 9, rarely 15 feet. Deciduous. Leaves to 2½ inches long. White or suffused with pink, very fragrant flowers in early July. Orange to bronze in autumn. −35 to −20° F.

OTHER SHRUBS TO TRY ARE:

Aesculus parviflora (bottle brush buckeye). Grows to 12 feet. Five to seven, nearly sessile, leaflets. Small white or pinkish flowers in panicles to 1 inch long in mid-July. −10 to −5° F.

*Andromeda polifolia** (bog-rosemary). Grows 1 to 2 feet. Creeping rootstocks. Oblong to linear leaves to 1½ inches long, with revolute margins. Flowers are white to pinkish, in small terminal clusters, and to ¼ inch in length. −50 to −35° F.

Aronia arbutifolia (red chokeberry). Grows to 10 feet. Gray leaves; white or reddish flowers less than ½ inch in diameter bloom in late May. Bright red berries, less than ½ inch in diameter in fall. Red leaves in the autumn. −20 to −10° F.

Calycanthus floridus (Carolina allspice). Grows to 10 feet. Ovate or elliptic leaves to 5 inches long, densely pubescent, and pale beneath; 2-inch flowers are dark reddish-brown. Yellowish in autumn. −20 to −10° F.

Ceanothus americanus (New Jersey Tea). Grows to 3 feet. Alternate ovate, and finely toothed leaves. Small white flowers in upright oblong clusters in mid-June. −20 to −10° F.

*C. velutinus** (snow bush). Grows to 15 feet. Alternate, elliptic, and finely toothed leaves, shining above and somewhat hairy beneath. White flowers. −5 to −10° F.

Cephalanthus occidentalis (buttonball bush). Grows to 20 feet. Ovate to oval-lanceolate leaves to 6 inches long, shining above. Creamy white flowers in round heads about 1 inch in diameter in late July. −20 to −10° F.

Clethra alnifolia (summersweet clethra). Grows to 10 feet. Ovate, obtuse, or acute leaves 4 inches long. Erect, usually panicled racemes. Yellow to orange in autumn. −35 to −20° F.

Cornus amomum (silky dogwood). Grows to 8 feet. Elliptical leaves. Creamy white flowers. Grows in wet places along streams. −30 to −20° F.

C. stolonifera (red osier dogwood). Grows to 10 feet. Dark red branches that spread by underground stems. Ovate or ovate-lanceolate leaves to 5 inches long. White or bluish flowers. −50 to −35° F.

Sambucus canadensis, *the blue elderberry, bears magnificent white flowers in June and July followed by blue-purple berries.* (USDA photo)

Corylus americana (American hazelnut). Grows to 10 feet. Leaves to 5 inches long, pubescent beneath. Two to six fruits; the involucre is about twice the length of the nut, with deep irregular lobes. −20 to −10° F.

Dirca palustris (leatherwood). Grows to 8 feet in rich moist woods. Very early yellow bloom in May-June. Good for shady spots, woods, or gardens along paths. −10 to −5° F.

Elaeagnus commutata (silverberry). Grows to 12 feet. Deciduous. Silvery leaves. One to three fragrant flowers in axils in May-June. Silvery fruit on very short stalks. Below −50° F.

Euonymus americanus (strawberry bush). Grows to 6 feet, in woods along stream banks. Leaves egg shaped and bright green. Flowers greenish-purple in May or June. −5 to 5° F.

Fothergilla gardenii (dwarf fothergilla). Grows to 3 feet. Ovate to oblong leaves with rounded or broadly cuneate base to 2 inches long; pale beneath. White flowers over 1 inch long in terminal spikes in mid-May. Brilliant yellow to scarlet in autumn. −10 to −5° F.

F. major (large fothergilla). Grows to 10 feet. Leaves to 4 inches long, pubescent beneath. White flowers with leaves in terminal flower spikes often 2 inches long in mid-May. Brilliant yellow to scarlet in autumn. −10 to −5° F.

F. monticola. Fragrant white flowers like bottlebrushes; good yellow fall color and for foundation plantings. Needs moisture. −5 to 5° F.

*Gaylussacia brachycera** (box huckleberry). Grows to 1½ feet. Evergreen foliage. Leaves to 1 inch long. White or pink, small, bell-shaped flowers in mid-May. Fruit is blue berry. −10 to −5° F.

Hamamelis vernalis (spring witch-hazel). Grows to 10 feet. Leaves to 5 inches long are nearly glabrous beneath. Yellow to reddish, ribbon-like, fragrant flowers to ½ inch long in January-March. Yellow in autumn. −10 to −5° F.

SHRUBS

MOCKORANGE   Philadelphus indorus

YAUPON   Ilex vomitoria

INKBERRY   Ilex glabra

CASCADES MAHONIA   Mahonia nervosa

H. virginiana (common witch-hazel). Grows to 15 feet. Leaves to 6 feet long, pubescent only on veins beneath. Yellow flowers with ribbonlike petals to ¾ inch long in early October. Yellow in autumn. −10 to −5° F.

Hydrangea arborescens (wild hydrangea). Grows to 10 feet. Ovate leaves, to 8 inches long, are glabrous or slightly pubescent beneath. White flowers in rounded or globular clusters to 6 inches across in June-July. −20 to −10° F.

H. arborescens 'Grandiflora' (hills of snow). Grows to 3 feet. White flowers in large rounded clusters about 6 inches in diameter in early July. −20 to −10° F.

H. quercifolia (oakleaf hydrangea). White summer flowers turn purplish with age. Dark red fall foliage. Needs shade. Good for house corners, and northern exposures. −5 to 5° F.

Hypericum kalmianum (shrubby St. John's wort). Bright yellow summer bloom even if tops winter-kill. Good for low informal hedge or fronting higher shrubs. Tolerates partial shade. −10 to −5° F.

*Ilex glabra** (inkberry). Grows to 9 feet. Lustrous foliage. Dark leaves to 2 inches. Inconspicuous, often solitary flowers (sexes separate) in mid-June. Fruit is small black berries ¼ inch in diameter in fall. −35 to −20° F.

I. verticillata (winterberry). Grows to 10 feet. Deciduous. Oval to lanceolate, toothed leaves, pubescent beneath, at least on nerves. Inconspicuous flowers (sexes separate) in June-July. Fruit is bright red berries, ¼ inch in diameter in fall and winter. −35 to −20° F.

*I. vomitoria** (yaupon), Can grow to 20 feet. Prefers sandy dunes. Leaves lustrous green. Flowers greenish-white in spring. Fruit is bright red in fall. 0 to 10° F.

Itea virginica (sweet spire). Grows to 10 feet. Deciduous. Finely toothed leaves to 4 inches long. White, fragrant flowers in upright

The fine Rhododendron catawbiense *is a delightful addition to any garden.* (Photo by Pat Matsumoto)

dense racemes 2 to 6 inches long in June-July. Brilliant red in autumn. −10 to −5° F.

*Kalmia latifolia** (mountain laurel). Grows to 30 feet. Evergreen foliage. Leaves to 5 inches long. Pink and white flowers in large clusters in mid-June. −35 to −20° F.

*Leucothoë catesbaei** (fetterbush). Grows to 6 feet. Shining ovate-lanceolate to lance-ovate leaves to 7 inches long. White flowers in racemes to 3 inches long in April-May. −20 to −10° F.

Lindera benzoin (spice bush). Grows to 15 feet. Deciduous. Oblong-ovate leaves to 5 inches long, turn yellow in autumn. Petiole usually less than ¾ inch long. Greenish-yellow, dense flowers in mid-April. Fruit is scarlet berries in early fall. −20 to −10° F.

*Mahonia aquifolium** (holly mahonia). Grows to 3, rarely 6 feet. Bronze to purplish in autumn. Semi to evergreen. Lustrous dark green foliage. Five to nine ovate leaflets to 3 inches long. Petioles to 2 inches long. Bright yellow flowers in spikes or pyramidal clusters in early May. Bluish-black fruitlike small grapes. *M. nervosa* (cascades mahonia), somewhat similar but smaller. −20 to −10° F.

*Myrica caroliniensis** (Northern bayberry). Grows to 9 feet. Ovate, deciduous or sometimes evergreen leaves, to 4 inches long. Does well in poor soil. Hardy to −50° F.

*M. pensylvanica** (bayberry). Grows to 9 feet. Deciduous or sometimes evergreen. Ovate, acute, or obtuse leaves to 4 inches long. Fruit is small gray berries (sexes separate) in fall and winter. Hardy to −50° F.

Philadelphus inodorus (mock orange). Grows to 10 feet growing on rocky slopes and along streams. Egg-shaped leaves pointed at tip. White flowers in May or June. Many garden varieties. −30 to −20° F.

*Pieris floribunda** (andromeda). Grows to 6 feet. Hairy branches. Ciliate leaves. White flowers in nodding pyramidal clusters to 4 inches high. Small fruitlike blueberries in late April. −20 to −10° F.

Potentilla fruticosa (shrubby cinquefoil). Growing in rocky or moist places, this 3-foot shrub has bright yellow flowers in June to September. −50 to −35° F.

Salix discolor (pussy willow). Grows to 20 feet. Oblong, wavy toothed, or nearly entire leaves to 4 inches long, glaucous beneath. Catkins appear before the leaves. −35 to −20° F.

Sambucus canadensis (American elder). Grows to 12 feet. Oval or lanceolate leaves. Leaflets to 6 inches long. Small white flowers in large flat clusters 6 to 8 inches in diameter in late June. Fruit is blue to black small berries in large clusters in late summer. −35 to −20° F.

Symphoricarpos albus (snowberry). Grows to 5 feet, on dog-wooded slopes and banks. Green, somewhat wavy leaves. Pink flowers May to July. Round white berries in fall. −20 to −10° F.

S. orbiculatus (Indian currant). Grows to 6 feet. Oval or ovate leaves to 2½ inches long, glaucous and usually pubescent beneath. Small, dense, yellowish white, and bell-shaped flowers, 1/6 inch long in May-June. Fruit is purplish-red, corallike berries in fall. −50 to −35° F.

Vaccinium corymbosum (swamp blueberry). Grows to 15 feet. Deciduous. Long, ovate-lanceolate leaves to 3 inches, glabrous to pubescent. White or pinkish flowers to ⅓ inch long in clusters in May. Fruit is blue-black berries. Scarlet in autumn, red twigs in winter. −35 to −20° F.

Viburnum acerifolium (maple-leaf viburnum). Grows to 6 feet. Three-lobed, maplelike, coarsely toothed leaves to 5 inches long. Yellowish to white small flowers in flat clusters in mid-June. Fruit is black berries in fall. Purplish in autumn. −35 to −20° F.

V. dentatum (arrowwood viburnum). Grows to 15 feet. Toothed glossy green foliage; creamy white flowers in clusters. Blue berries in fall. −50 to −35° F.

V. lantana (hobble bush). Grows to 15 feet. Ovate, finely toothed leaves to 5 inches long. White flowers to 4 inches across in May-June. Red fruit turns black. −35 to −20° F.

V. lentago (nanny berry). Grows to 30 feet. Ovate, finely toothed leaves to 4 inches long. White flowers in flat clusters to 5 inches across in late May. Fruit is black berries in fall and winter. Purplish red in autumn. −25 to −20° F.

V. prunifolium (black haw). Grows to 15 feet. Ovate or broad-oval, finely toothed leaves to 3 inches long. White flowers in flat clusters to 4 inches across in mid-May. Fruit is blue-black berries in fall. Shining red in autumn. −35 to −20° F.

V. trilobum (American cranberry bush). Grows to 12 feet. Broad, ovate, three-lobed, and coarsely toothed leaves to 5 inches long. White flowers in flat clusters to 4 inches across in May-June. (Flowers are sterile.) Fruit is scarlet, berries in fall and winter. −35 to −20° F.

* Evergreen

8. Vines and Ground Covers ✐

Vines and ground covers offer a gardener more than meets the eye. Lovely climbing and cascading vines are great disguises for unsightly areas, garden houses, porches, walls, or fences. These plants soften the sometime sterile lines of today's architecture and are desirable if strategically placed.

Remember, however, that vines are climbing plants and will smother anything that gets in their way. Some vines climb by tendrils or stems; others have clinging pads that can cover even bare walls. Forget vines on any surface that needs periodic painting because it is simply too much trouble to extricate them from a surface once they get going. And even if you install them on trellises in front of a house wall they eventually find their way to the wall.

Vines grow quickly, which might be an advantage or a disadvantage, depending on your garden, but none should be allowed to grow rampant. Most vines need periodic pruning to keep them looking good and within bounds. Start pruning and keeping vines in bounds when they first start growing, and continue the pruning every month. Once they get started, overgrown vines can be pretty troublesome to prune.

Plant woody vines in a deep planting hole at the same level they were growing in the nursery (at least three feet deep) so roots will have growing room. Replace with fresh soil, and tamp down so there are no air pockets. Leave a depression in soil around the plant to facilitate watering.

There are many desirable native vines, but there are a few that you certainly don't want in the garden, e.g. poison ivy and bindweed

Confederate violet (Viola priceana) *mingles with sweet woodruff* (Asperula odorata) *between a rhododendron* (TOP) *and skimmia* (RIGHT). (Photo by Marjorie Dietz)

(convolvulus). The morning glory too is apt to be a pest and smothers other plants; it is very difficult to get rid of them. Here are some popular vines to try:

Aristolochia durior (Dutchman's pipe). This can grow to 30 feet with little trouble and is perfect for covering arbors and trellises. The big dark green, heart-shaped leaves are attractive, but the unique flowers are more bizarre than beautiful. Needs a good soil to prosper but will grow in either sun or shade. −20 to −10° F.

Bignonia (flame vine). Also called clystoma in the trade. A really lovely vine with magnificent red- or violet-streaked funnel flowers. Slow to start, bignonia eventually covers fast and provides a lush frame of leaves. It's invasive and will crawl over anything, yet in the right situation it is a superlative plant. Can grow to 100 feet. It will grow in a rich or a poor soil, but it must have intense sun to thrive. −20 to −10° F.

Celastrus scandens (false bittersweet). Orange-yellow flowers and handsome foliage make bittersweet a good vine selection. Plants grow in almost any garden soil in shade or in sun. Do not place near trees or vine will eventually take over. −50 to −35° F.

Aristolochia durior, *Dutchman's pipe, is a woody, quick-climbing vine with handsome foliage.* (Photo by Molly Adams)

Clematis virginiana (clematis). Graceful leaves and handsome groups of white flowers make this a desirable vine for your garden. Likes a somewhat acid soil and partial sunny place where it can grow to 10 feet or more. Other clematis species are also worth trying but hard to find. −20 to −10° F.

Gelsemium sempervirens (Carolina yellow jessamine). A fine dark green vine that sprouts lovely yellow blooms. Grows vigorously and makes a nice display. For partial sun and average soils. −5 to 5° F.

Lonicera (honeysuckle). Several species are available, and perhaps *L. sempervirens*, with handsome green leaves and tubular, scarlet or orange flowers, is best. A vigorous grower, this vine will need a strong support. Grows readily in partial shade. −35 to −20° F.

Parthenocissus quinquefolia (Virginia creeper). Compound leaves that turn red in fall make this a worthwhile addition to the garden picture. It is a fine subject for covering walls or buildings. Grows in either sun or shade and in almost any kind of soil. −35 to −20° F.

Passiflora incarnata (wild passion flower). A handsome vine with exquisite blue or white flowers that bloom one after another all summer. Needs a humusy soil and sun. −5 to 5° F.

Vitis (grape). There are grapes for various zones; more people should grow them. The leaves are quite decorative. The vine grows quickly and needs little attention. Check to see if your local dealers have it.

Ground covers have been steadily gaining popularity, and some specialized books about them have appeared recently. Ground covers are an easy way to make gardening simple; they cover an area with lovely foliage, are relatively easy to grow, and, most importantly, they crowd out weeds. Furthermore, they increase rapidly if you need good coverage.

Ground-cover installation is simple: make planting pockets of three to four inches and insert seedlings. Spacing is a matter of

NATIVE GROUND-COVERING VINES

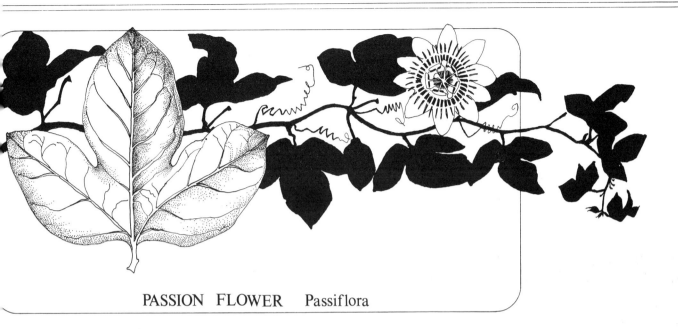

PASSION FLOWER   Passiflora

CAROLINA YELLOW JESSAMINE
Gelsemium sempervirens

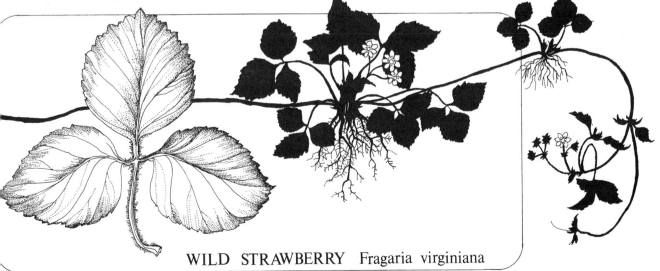

WILD STRAWBERRY   Fragaria virginiana

opinion, but do not put them too close to each other. Give them room to spread because they will proliferate easily.

Where it is difficult to establish a lawn or where there are hills or ravines, ground covers are immensely popular. The plants are excellent for binding sandy soil and for checking erosion in hills. Some ground covers need shade; others tolerate full sun and even drought. In cold-weather areas, start plants in the spring. Where

A delightful ground cover is Gaultheria procumbens *in top section of this planter box. Commonly called wintergreen, the berries are highly fragrant. (Photo by author)*

winters are moderate, fall or spring is the planting time. Here are some of the best plants to use as ground cover:

Andromeda polifolia (bog rosemary). Low evergreen to about 12 inches. Narrow leaves and pinkish flowers. Prefers shade.

Arctostaphylos uva-ursi (bearberry). A popular creeping ground cover in the West. Ornamental with lustrous leaves and red berries and grows easily in sun and almost any soil.

Asarum canadense. Lovely dark green broad leaves. Makes a handsome mat to 16 inches. Needs partial shade.

Convallaria majalis (lily-of-the-valley). Apple-green foliage and fragrant white flowers. Will tolerate sun or shade. Forms dense beds.

Coptis trifolia (goldthread). A small creeper that likes a shady moist situation. Stays evergreen if protected in winter.

Fragaria vesca (strawberry). A quickly spreading ground cover that will grow in sun or shade in almost any soil. Invasive, so use with caution.

Galax aphylla. A stemless evergreen with heart-shaped leaves that turn beautiful scarlet in fall. Needs a shady situation.

Gaultheria procumbens (wintergreen). Spatula-shaped small leaves turning red in fall. Scarlet berries. Prefers shade.

Gaylussacia brachycera (box huckleberry). A good creeping evergreen that should be used more.

Hypericum species (St. John's wort). A large group of native plants. Yellow flowered and generally small. Also classed as shrubs. Plants are easily grown; most prefer shady situation.

Juniperus horizontalis (creeping juniper). A favorite ground cover. Bluish-green, and handsome. Grow in somewhat sunny location.

Gelsemium sempervirens, *Carolina yellow jessamine, decorates the fence in the author's garden.* (Photo by author)

Mitchella repens (partridgeberry). Long, dark green leaves with white lines. Red berries. Excellent ground cover in shade.

Phlox subulata (moss pink). Perennials, forming mats to 6 inches tall. Lovely white to pink flowers. Makes excellent cover in a sunny location.

Sanguinaria canadensis (bloodroot). Handsome green leaves and exquisite flowers in early spring. Takes shade.

Trilliums (many kinds). A large group, with handsome leaves and flowers. Easy to grow once they become established. Most thrive in shade, some in full sun. Good drainage is essential.

FERN GARDEN

9. Fern Gardens ✿

I think that garden ferns are perhaps the most underrated plants. Yet even the smallest area of ferns offers a quiet, secluded, green glen—cool and lovely—that can grace almost any property where there is some shade. Ferns have a great diversity in form and size, and green is simply not green. For example, some ferns have dark green fronds, others are light green, and still others are apple green.

There are native ferns for almost any wild garden (except in the desert), and in the right location they are amenable plants. Ferns will grow in poor or rich soil, dry or moist places, and although most do prefer shade, some will grow in a limited amount of sunlight. Once planted in your garden, ferns will come up every year; indeed, it is hard to kill them once they are established. So for any neglected shady area in your garden, do consider these fine plants. The fern garden, like any good garden, needs planning, because it should be part of the landscape rather than an isolated area. There are so many ferns and they come in so many different sizes that it is well to know something about them before planning the garden. Group together ferns of the same size rather than a small one with a large one (that creates a spotty effect). Consider texture; for example, some ferns, like the maidenhairs, are delicate and lacy, while ferns such as blechnum are stiff and bold. It is quite all right to use contrasting textures together, but, as mentioned, choose plants of similar size. Set groups of ferns near each other to achieve a harmonious picture. The fern garden is a natural place for woodland plants such as trilliums, may apples, Dutchman's breeches, violets, and others. Furthermore, most ferns do not attain full growth for six to eight weeks after

109

spring, so the wild flowers can live harmoniously with them, one taking over when the other finishes blooming. Many ferns last until frost, and the hardy types remain throughout winter.

Make a plan on paper. Locate the fern garden under trees with adequate shade. The plants should look as if they have always been there, rather than just planted. In time they will establish themselves and provide a green glen that is an asset to any property.

To get ferns off to a good start, dig about twelve inches or more, break up soil, and add leaf mold and compost. Strive for a rich humusy soil. Some ferns such as the chain and lady ferns need an acid soil, so work in oak leaves or wood chips. For ferns like maidenhair spleenworts, add limestone to provide the soil with alkali.

Put a few small pebbles in place to anchor the roots; do not add any fertilizer. Try to do fern planting in the early fall. Space medium size ferns one to two feet apart, larger ones three feet apart. Keep the soil loose, never packed solidly.

A good leaf mulch is necessary for good fern growth, but never use rakes or hoes—be sure the plants have a leaf-covered soil because this will do wonders for them and save you work. Commercial fer-

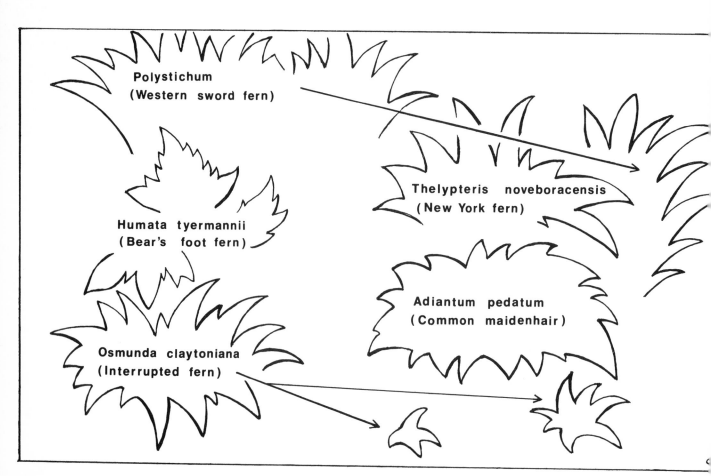

KEY TO FERN GARDEN

Here, all kinds of native ferns lead the way to the house in the background.
(Photo by Molly Adams)

tilizers are generally too strong for ferns, so no supplemental feeding is necessary. Occasionally sprinkle humus and compost on the
soil, and in fall add a light layer of bone meal. Keep the soil around
the ferns well watered; light mistings are harmful, so water copi-
ously, especially during dry spells.

The following table lists the best ferns and their growing
conditions:

NAME	LEAF	SOIL	LIGHT
Adiantum pedatum (American maidenhair fern)	Soft, light to medium green. Forked and diverging.	Rich humus constantly moist.	Medium shade.
Asplenium platyneuron (ebony spleenwort)	Deep green, slender, double tapering.	Loose, woodland soil.	Medium shade to alternate sunlight.
A. trichomanes (maidenhair spleenwort)	Deep green, slender.	Humus with small pieces of limestone. Requires good drainage.	Medium shade to alternate sunlight.
Botrychium virginianum (rattlesnake fern)	Yellow-green to rich green.	Rich, moist, woodland soil, neutral to slightly acid.	Medium to deep shade.
Camptosorus rhizophyllus (walking fern)	Medium green, elongate, tapering.	Grows best between limestone rocks. Avoid overwatering.	Shade to alternate sunlight.
Cystopteris fragilis (fragile bladder fern)	Medium or green.	Loose neutral soil.	Shade to alternate sunlight.

Lacy ferns are welcome additions to gardens; this close-up shows the intricate tapestry of fronds. (Photo by J. Barnich)

FERNS

COMMON MAIDENHAIR
Adiantum pedatum

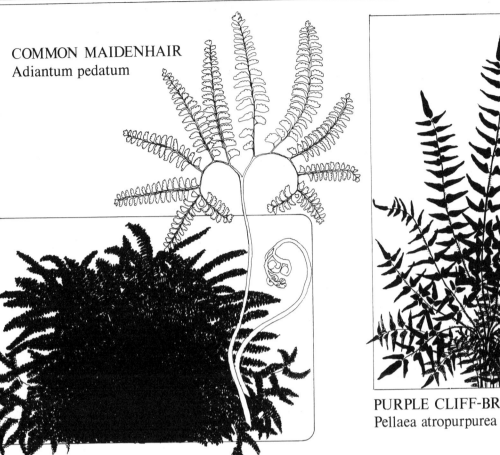

PURPLE CLIFF-BRAKE
Pellaea atropurpurea

FRAGILE BLADDER FERN
Cystopteris fragilis

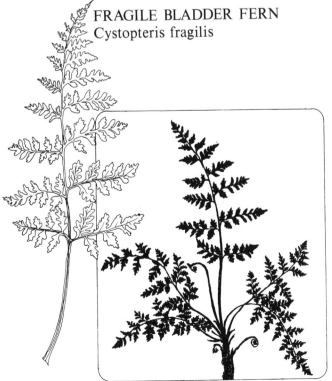

SENSITIVE FERN
Onoclea sensibilis

This lovely garden has its share of ferns; they mingle beautifully with other plants and provide grace and beauty. (Photo by Ken Molino)

NAME	LEAF	SOIL	LIGHT
Dryopteris cristata	Dark green, leathery, erect.	Slightly acid, constantly damp, loose woodland mulch.	Open to deep shade.
D. goldiana (Goldie's fern)	Deep green, leathery.	Rich humus, constantly moist.	Cool, open to medium shade.
D. intermedia	Deep green.	Deep, rocky soil rich in humus. Neutral or slightly acid.	Open to medium shade.
Onoclea sensibilis (sensitive fern)	Yellow-green to green.	Neutral or subacid, moist.	Open shade. Tolerates full sunlight if in marshy area.
Osmunda cinnamomea (cinnamon fern)	Yellow-green to deep waxy green.	Acid, constantly damp.	Open shade.
O. claytoniana (interrupted fern)	Yellow-green to waxy green.	Acid, constantly moist.	Open shade to alternate sunlight in damper soil.
O. regalis v. 'spectabilis'	Deep green.	Highly acid, constantly moist.	Shade to alternate sunlight when growing in bogs.
Pellaea atropurpurea (purple cliff-brake)	Gray-green.	Slightly alkaline.	Open shade to alternate sunlight.
Polypodium virginianum (common polypody)	Yellow-green to medium green.	Moist to slightly acid. Tolerates short dry periods.	Open shade to alternate sunlight.
Polystichum acrostichoides (Christmas fern)	Various shades of green, darkening with age.	Moist, stony woodland, mulch.	Open shade. Tolerates some direct sunlight where moisture is sufficient.
Thelypteris noveboracensis (New York fern)	Yellow-green to medium green.	Humusy acid.	Will tolerate sun, but shade best. Deciduous.

NAME	LEAF	SOIL	LIGHT
Woodwardia areolata	Glossy, medium to dark green.	Acid soil.	Open shade. Tolerates considerable sunlight when in moist soil.
W. virginica	Deep green to yellow-green, depending on light.	Acid soil.	Open shade. Tolerates considerable sunlight when in moist soil.

10. Orchids

It certainly is possible to grow wild orchids in your garden, as a friend of mine in Chicago proved—he grew some of the loveliest wildlings you would ever want to see. Most people are familiar with the corsage orchids, but there are a host of other orchids, the wild orchids that are free from the hand of man. These wild orchids are distributed throughout the United States: Florida, Georgia, Michigan, Wisconsin, and so forth. They are such beautiful flowers, it is a shame that so few native stands still exist, so it is most important to perpetuate the species and grow them in our gardens. Because most of the plants are available from suppliers, do *not*, under any circumstances, take them from the woods.

The orchids we are most familiar with are the ladyslippers (Cypripediums), but there are other excellent, lesser-known orchids. Habenarias, frequently offered by suppliers, have crowns of spectacular flowers with fringed lips and long spurs. *Calopogon pulchellus*, called the grass pink, offers brilliant lavender flowers. *Spiranthes cernua*, (nodding ladies' treasure) blooms in summer with white flowers.

In nature, most of the terrestrial orchids grow in low wet ground in mainly shady situations because they like cool wet feet. Some, however, will tolerate more sun and grow in grassy situations where it may be quite dry or quite wet. In your garden, make sure orchids have a really moist soil, coolness, and, for the most part, shade.

Ladyslippers, as noted, are the most popular natives and offer breathtaking flowers. They are somewhat stringent in their requirements, and most require an acid soil. However, once established they

118

soon multiply, and it is possible to have a stand of orchids in a few years if they are carefully tended. Here are the most popular lady-slippers:

Cypripedium acaule (pink ladyslipper). Pink blooms. Needs acid soil and shade. Common and widespread.

C. candidum (small white ladyslipper). Lovely white flowers. Likes some sun and a slightly alkaline soil. Native to New York State, and New Jersey, and westward to Missouri.

C. parviflorum. Smaller yellow flowers, and generally confused with *C. pubescens*. Needs same conditions.

C. pubescens. Large yellow flowers on wand stems. Needs slightly acid soil and light shade. Needs much watering. Has extensive range.

A popular woodland orchid is rattlesnake plantain, Goodyera pubescens. *It has green and white leaves and bears greenish-white flowers; needs acid soil.* (Photo by Marjorie Dietz)

Cypripedium pubescens, *a wild orchid, is right at home in this city woodland garden.* (Photo by Pat Matsumoto)

C. reginae (showy ladyslipper). One of the most beautiful orchids, with pink and white lip. Needs cool, moist conditions, light shade, and slightly acid soil. Give it plenty of water. Native to northern New England as well as Georgia, Tennessee, and Missouri.

OTHER NATIVE ORCHIDS INCLUDE:

Calopogon pulchellus (grass pink orchid). Grassy leaves and incredibly lovely purple, flat-faced flowers on tall wands. A prairie native.

Calypso bulbusa. Fast vanishing. This exquisite beauty bears an erect simple blossom of lavender hue. Occasionally available from suppliers.

Epicactus gigantea (stream orchid). Native to the Western mountains. Bears fanciful multicolored blooms, several to a stalk.

Goodyera pubescens (downy rattlesnake plantain). Common throughout the Eastern states. Desirable for its variegated leaves rather than for its tiny flowers.

Habenaria psycodes (small purple fringed orchid). Native to northern New England and the higher Appalachians. A fringed beauty that would do any gardener proud.

Orchis spectabilis (showy orchid). Native to Tennessee, Georgia, and Missouri. Bears a white and pink flower. Grows in moist woods.

Pogonia ophioglossoides (goldcrest orchid). Widely distributed in cool bogs and wet grasslands. Bears pink and gold flowers.

Close-up view of Cypripedium pubescens showing its lovely flower form and handsome foliage. (Photo by Pat Matsumoto)

11. Keep It Beautiful ✐

Once your garden is growing and glowing with colorful plants, you'll want to keep it that way. A certain amount of care will be necessary to keep plants healthy and thriving; this entails pruning, weeding, grooming, and cleaning. It is wise to do these duties a little at a time but *all the time* rather than waiting for months and then tackling an overgrown garden.

In addition to maintenance, you'll want to be sure plants are free of pests and growing instead of just existing. Posionous sprays are not necessary if you allow the garden to grow naturally and use organic controls. You will never have a completely insect-free garden, but you will never be poisoning land and perhaps yourself.

MAINTENANCE
Special tools, equipment, power mowers, and sweepers are not necessary unless you are overly fond of machinery and expense. Generally, such basic tools as trowels, spading forks, spades, rakes, and hoes will take care of all the necessary chores. And don't forget a wheelbarrow for moving soil or plants. Do weeding, cultivation of soil, and planting on a regular basis rather than letting the garden get ahead of you. Of course, at vacation time, if you can't get someone to tend the garden while you are away, you will have to catch up on maintenance upon your return.

OPPOSITE: *The shrubs and trees around this lovely patio garden have been deftly pruned and groomed; the overall effect is charming.* (Photo by Ken Molino)

Keep plants and the property clear of debris because more insect eggs, insects, and disease, start from unsanitary conditions. Observe and remove dead twigs and leaves on a regular basis. If insects appear, use natural controls as outlined in this chapter.

Pruning is an essential part of good gardening because it helps shape plants, promotes growth, and contributes to the general good looks of the landscape. Ill-shaped trees and overgrown shrubs are easily seen in winter when foliage has fallen. Prune away dead branches and diseased limbs as soon as you notice them to protect other plants in the garden from disease. Use sharp tools, and cut cleanly. Afterward, apply wound paint to wounds on trees and shrubs so bacteria cannot enter the tree or shrub.

When pruning trees, cut out crisscrossed branches, and keep an open framework. Cut branches flush with the trunk; do not leave stubs, and never prune when wood is frozen or brittle. Let professionals handle large shade trees, because it is too hazardous to attempt it yourself.

Shrubs that flower on previous years' wood can be pruned im-

This woodland path to the house is too natural; even nature needs a helping hand from time to time. Trees should be pruned, shrubs cleared to remedy the jungle look. (Photo by author)

Pruning is a necessary part of good gardening and should not be neglected even in the native garden. (Photo by Seymour Smith and Sons)

mediately after they bloom in spring or summer. Cut away weak wood, and let light and air circulate so the plant can grow freely in the next season. Shrubs that flower on current wood need pruning in winter or very early spring.

Follow these six rules for pruning:

1. *After making a cut, apply wound paint.*
2. *Don't leave stubs infection might enter.*
3. *Cut away crossed branches, on small trees.*
4. *Don't let a main trunk divide into a fork—remove one branch.*
5. *Always prune slightly above a bud.*
6. *Always wear gloves, and use sturdy ladders and clean sharp tools.*

A good garden "snips" is necessary to keep plants looking good and to promote health. (Photo courtesy Tru-Temper)

INSECT PREVENTION*

You will never win the war against pests and blight, but you can keep trouble to a minimum by being observant and by using safe controls (including natural predators such as birds and insects) when necessary. Inspect stems and leaves frequently to be sure that pests aren't getting a foothold, for once entrenched they are tough to get rid of. While massing for an attack, however, they can be eradicated without resorting to strong poisons.

* This section from Jack Kramer, *Garden Planning for the Small Property*, New York, Charles Scribner's Sons, 1972.

Persistent chlorinated hydrocarbon insecticides are harmful to the world ecosystem because they remain in the chain of nature and so should not be used. These include products that contain Aldrin, Chlordane, DDT, Dieldrin, Endrin, Heptachlor, Kelthane, Lindane, Methoxychlor, Tedion, and Toxaphene (not a complete list). Botanical repellents made from plants, such as pyrethrum and rotenone, are generally preferable to the synthetic poisons in fighting insects. If necessary, some of the synthetics such as Malathion and Sevin might have to be used in the battle of the bugs, but they are still poisons and should be handled with great respect. Of course, nonpoisonous controls—dormant oils, plain water, and natural predators such as birds, lacewings, ladybugs, and praying mantises—are the best controls. Insects are now available from insectaries, listed in gardening magazines.

Most insects that attack gardens can be seen, and for the most part are easily subdued. Some pests, of course, are microscopic, but the damage they do can be seen readily in leaves and stems.

Fungi and bacteria that produce plant disease also produce symp-

Ladybugs are excellent insect predators and will keep a garden aphid-free. (USDA photo)

toms—visible clues in the appearance of the plant. Keep a watchful eye for signs of trouble in the garden and catch it before it starts.

Chewing insects, like cutworms, caterpillars, some beetles, and leaf rollers, cause considerable damage by chewing stems and foliage. Synthetics such as Diazinon and Carbaryl (Sevin) will take care of most of these pests. For sucking insects like aphid, scale, mealybug, and red spiders that pierce the foliage and take juices from the stems and leaves, use pyrethrum; if this doesn't work, Malathion is an alternate control.

Snails and slugs are ugly pests that chew holes in leaves, but they are easily controlled. Use one of the snail-baits that contains metaldehyde, but do not apply any metaldehyde products that contain arsenicals.

With all pesticides check labels carefully to see what the product really contains and avoid the persistent hydrocarbons, as mentioned earlier.

Fungus diseases are unsightly infections, such as black spots on leaves and crow rot on leaves that turn gray and watery. Dust plants with sulfur and reduce moisture considerably. Botrytis blight causes gray mold on foliage and flowers; it is best to discard the infected plants. Also discard plants that develop spots, circles, or streaks of black, silver, or green on leaves or stalks. These marks may be caused by virus, and it is better to destroy plants than to cope with the unknown.

With diseased plants, send adequate specimens of the plant with a written explanation to your state agricultural experimental station for diagnosis and treatment. (See Appendix for listings.)

12. Native Plants in Terrariums 🌿

Miniature landscapes of native plants in terrariums (closed containers) offer hours of fascinating viewing. There is something infinitely charming about plants in their own little world, especially if the landscape scene simulates natural habitats. You can duplicate a woodland landscape, create a miniature bog, or have a rocky ledge for tiny ferns. There are endless possibilities, which is one reason why the terrarium is such a popular garden.

Another advantage of miniature glass gardens is that you can grow native plants that would not survive in average home conditions. In a closed container, these forest inhabitants thrive because they are protected from drafts and fluctuating temperatures. The terrarium can be almost any type of glass container, from a brandy snifter to a goldfish bowl or an aquarium. Also on the market are plastic bowls and special terrarium kits manufactured by various companies. The terrarium, whether it is bowl or a tank, is generally covered with a piece of glass to ensure humidity for plants and to provide an evenly moist soil. Some ventilation, however, will be needed from time to time; if you see the glass clouding with excess moisture, lift the lid for a few hours so air can circulate within the garden.

Wild plants in a terrarium can, of course, be of any type; there seems to be an endless variety of shade-loving woodland denizens for the glass container. Basically, however, woodland subjects such as partridge berry, rattlesnake plantain, hepaticas, and lycopodiums are used.

When you are landscaping the terrarium, remember that the *center* is the focal point; place tall plants in the rear and smaller ones up front. Use mosses and low-growing covers to make the scene as natural as possible. Small rocks are perfect for height and ledges, and tiny pebbles for paths are suitable.

Use rich leafy soil. I use one-third leaf mold, one-third humus, and one-third porous stones. *Don't* use packaged soils (they are generally too heavy) or soil-less mixes (plants in them require constant feeding.

Plants in terrariums depend on a balanced environment of the

Striped pipsissewa (LEFT), *goldthread* (CENTER), *and partridgeberry* (RIGHT) *are excellent woodland plants for terrariums.* (Photo by author)

proper humidity, temperature, and light. Soil should be evenly moist but never soggy because a soggy soil coupled with too much heat or darkness may create fungus disease. So keep your garden cool (about 55° F. at night), and lift the lid or cover occasionally to let air circulate in the growing area. Occasionally trim and snip plants to keep them shapely and attractive. Pick off faded flowers and decayed leaves immediately.

WOODLAND PLANTS TO USE

The following plants are ideal for the woodland terrarium:

Calopogon pulchellus (grass pink orchid). Fine orchid with handsome flowers.

Caltha palustris (marsh marigold). Lovely yellow flowers. A real charmer.

Chimaphila maculata (striped pipsissewa). Handsome variegated foliage.

C. umbellata (common pipsissewa). Leaves resemble the groundcover pachysandra.

Chiogenes hispidula (creeping snowberry). Shiny leaves on a creeping vine. Fragrant. Must have coolness.

Coptis trifolia (goldthread). Four inches tall, with cloverlike leaves and waxy white flowers. Prefers cold, damp conditions.

Darlingtonia californica (California pitcher). Native to northern California and the Oregon coast. Droopy, unusual flowers and cylindrical, bizarre leaves. Large, to 28 inches, but unusual and worth space.

Epigaea repens (trailing arbutus). A longtime favorite. Cheerful creeper with woody, hairy stems and green leaves. Delightful, fragrant, bell-shaped flowers.

Goodyera pubescens (downy rattlesnake plantain). Woodland orchid with curiously marked leaves.

Hepatica americana. Maroon-tined foliage; dainty blue blooms. Common in Midwest.

Mitchella repens (partridge berry). Red berries, and grassy-green leaves make this a stellar plant.

Pyrola elliptica (shinleaf or wintergreen). Oval green leaves. Does not like as much moisture as other bog plants.

Sarracenia purpurea (Northern pitcher plant). Insectivorous plant. Somewhat large, but so different that it is worth space. Hollow "pitcher" leaves, and bizarre flowers.

Small ferns too belong in the woodland scene; there are dozens to choose from. (Photo by author)

Viola (violets). Many fine species will flourish in a terrarium. Especially good ones are *V. palmata* (wood violet) and *V. fimbriatula* (wooly blue violet).

FERNS

The fern family is large and varied. We are familiar with Boston ferns and bird's-nest ferns as house plants, but lesser-known ferns are seldom seen in the home. In covered gardens, where it is cool, shady, and moist, these plants will charm you. They cannot be beat for their decorative appeal—most are lacy, fresh, and crisp, in lovely shades of green. The following ferns are usually available from suppliers:

Adiantum (maidenhair fern). Many varieties of this beautiful fern; use small seedlings. Generally dormant in winter, these plants may

This terrarium houses some woodland plants along with graceful ferns. (Photo by author)

Terrariums are not restricted to aquarium containers; this woodland garden is in a plexiglass case. (Photo by author)

grow all year in a case. *A. cuneatum gracillimum* has delicate lacy fronds, and *A. pedatum* (American maidenhair) has graceful curved fronds.

Asplenium (spleenwort). Ideal, easy-to-grow plants for glass gardens. Prefer shade and neutral soil. *A. platyneuron* (ebony spleenwort) is about 12 inches tall. Feathery fronds with brownish-purple stems. *A. trichomanes* (maidenhair spleenwort) grows to 6 inches. Thick clustered fronds with 1 inch leaflets on black ribs. *A. ruta-muraria* (wall rue) grows to 4 inches. Tough and leathery dark-green fronds.

Blechnum. Good ferns for a large case. Revel in a saturated atmosphere and partial shade. Use young plants. Try *B. spicant* (deer fern) —either dark and glossy evergreen fronds and is easy to grow.

Botrychium (grape fern). Found in open woods with moderate moisture. Grows to about 20 inches. Young seedlings prosper in covered gardens. Try *B. virginianum* (rattlesnake fern).

Camptosorus rhyzophyllus (walking fern). Diminutive charmer with small evergreen fronds. Plants root at the tips and "walk" over the soil.

Cyrtomium (holly fern). Sturdy and shiny, with stiff fronds.

Dryopteris (wood fern). Grows in damp places. Dark green plants, variable in size. *D. cristata* has evergreen blue-green fronds. *D. linnaeana* (oak fern) is sometimes classified as *Polypodium dryopteris*.

Pellaea rotundifolia (button fern). Blue-green fronds with rolled edges and fuzzy brown root stock in a globular mass. Does not like temperature changes.

Polypodium (polypody). A group of handsome ferns that thrive in shade and moisture. Easy to grow; and charming. *P. vulgare* (common polypody) has evergreen fronds, and grows to about 8 inches. Likes coolness.

Polystichum. Shade-loving group; very decorative. *P. setifera* (hedge fern) has feathery fronds covered with brown hairlike scales.

Pteris (brake). Delightful, tiny ferns. Several kinds. Ideal glass-case plants and vigorous growers. *P. cretica* (ribbon fern) has delicate fronds to about 8 inches; *P. ensiformis* has silver and green fronds.

APPENDIX:

Plant Sources
Books to Read
Where You Can See Native Plants
Conservation Groups
Agricultural Extension Service

Plant Sources

Arthur Eames Allgrove   (mostly plants)
North Wilmington, Mass. 01887

Clyde Robin   (seed and plants)
P. O. Box 2091
Castro Valley, Calif. 94546

Dauber's Nurseries   (mostly trees and shrubs)
P. O. Box 1746
York, Pa. 17405

George W. Park Seed Co.   (seeds and plants)
Greenwood, S.C. 29646

Harry E. Saier   (seeds and plants)
Dimondale, Mich. 48821

Lamb Nurseries   (mostly plants)
E. 101 Sharp Ave.
Spokane, Wash. 99202

Leslie's Wildflower Nursery   (seeds and plants)
30 Summer St.
Methuen, Mass. 01844

Lounsberry Gardens   (mostly plants)
P. O. Box 135
Oakford, Ill. 62673

Mincemoyer Nursery   (mostly plants)
Rt. 5, Box 379
Jackson, N.J. 08527

Musser Forests   (mostly trees and shrubs)
Box 73
Indiana, Pa. 15701

P. de Jager and Sons   (mostly bulbs)
188 Asbury St.
South Hamilton, Mass. 01982

W. Atlee Burpee Co.   (mostly seed)
Philadelphia, Pa. 19132

Walter Marx Gardens   (mostly bulbs)
Boring, Ore. 97009

Books to Read

A Woodland Garden, A. T. Johnson, Country Life Ltd., London, and
     Charles Scribner's Sons, New York, 1937.

Bluebells and Bittersweet, Bebe Miles, Van Nostrand Reinhold Co.,
     New York, 1968.

Discover American Trees, Rutherford Platt, Dodd, Mead & Co., New
     York, 1968.

Gardening with Native Plants, Brooklyn Botanic Gardens, Handbook
     #38, Brooklyn, New York, 1962.

Gardens Under Glass, Jack Kramer, Simon & Schuster, New York,
     1968.

How to Recognize Shrubs, William Grimm, Stackpole Books, Harrisburg, Pa., 1966.

Ornamental American Shrubs, William R. Van Depal, Oxford University Press, New York, 1942.

Plant Propagation, Principles and Practice, Hudson T. Hartmann and Dale E. Kester, Prentice Hall, Inc., Englewood Cliffs, N.J., 1959.

Shrubs and Vines for American Gardens, Donald Wyman, Macmillan, New York, 1969.

The Gardener's Fern Book, F. Gordon Foster, Hawthorn Books Inc., New York, 1970.

Trees for American Gardens, Donald Wyman, Macmillan, New York, 1968.

Wild Flowers, H. D. House, Macmillan, New York, 1942.

Wild Flowers for Your Garden, Helen S. Hull, Gramercy Publications, New York, 1942.

Wildflowers of North America, Robert S. Lemmon and Charles C. Johnson, Hanover House, Garden City, N.Y., 1961.

Wildflowers of the United States (in 5 volumes), Harold William Rickett, McGraw-Hill Inc., New York, 1971:
    Wild Flowers of the Northeastern States
    Wild Flowers of the Northwestern States
    Wild Flowers of the Southeastern States
    Wild Flowers of the Southwestern States
    Wild Flowers of Texas

*Where You Can See Native Plants**

The following is a partial listing of gardens and arboretums throughout the United States where native plants are grown. Write or call for admission charges and times.

Arboretum of the University of Alabama
Box 1927
Tuscaloosa, Alabama 35486

Arizona-Sonora Desert Museum and
    Demonstration Garden
Box 5607, Tucson Mt. Park
Tucson, Arizona 85703

Boyce Thompson Southwestern Arboretum
Box 307
Superior, Arizona 85273

Desert Botanical Garden of Arizona
6400 E. McDowell Rd.
Box 5415
Phoenix, Arizona 85010

Encanto Park
1900 N. 15th Avenue
Phoenix, Arizona 85010

Botanic Garden
University of California
Los Angeles, California 90054

Golden Gate Park
San Francisco, California 94122

Huntington Botanical Gardens
1151 Oxford Rd.
San Marino, California 91108

Santa Barbara Botanic Garden, Inc.
1212 Mission Canyon Rd.
Santa Barbara, California 93105

* Compiled from the 1971 Directory of Amercian Horticulture Handbook published by the American Horticultural Society (Alexandria, Virginia).

Connecticut Arboretum at Connecticut
  College
Connecticut College
Box 1511
New London, Connecticut 06320

Kenilworth Aquatic Gardens
Douglas St. N.E.
Washington, D.C. 20250

Highlands Hammock State Park
Box 669
Sebring, Florida 33870

University of Georgia Botanical Garden
Room 200, Barrow Hall
University of Georgia
Athens, Georgia 30601

Charles Huston Shattuck Arboretum
College of Forestry
University of Idaho
Moscow, Idaho 83843

Botanic Garden of the Chicago
  Horticultural Society
775 Dundee Rd.
Box 90
Glencoe, Illinois 60022

Morton Arboretum
Rt. 53
Lisle, Illinois

Hayes Regional Arboretum
801 Elks Rd.
Richmond, Indiana 47374

Honeywell Gardens
Box 432
Wabash, Indiana 46992

University of Northern Iowa Gardens
Cedar Falls, Iowa 50613

Bernheim Forest Arboretum
Clermont, Kentucky 40110

Fay Hyland Botanical Plantation
317 Deering Hall
University of Maine
Orono, Maine 04473

Thuya Gardens
Asticou Terrace
Northeast Harbor, Maine 04662

Wild Gardens of Acadia
Acadia National Park
Sieur de Monts Spring
Bar Harbor, Maine 04609

Alexandra Botanic Garden & Hunnewell
   Arboretum
Wellesley State College
Wellesley, Massachusetts 02101

Garden in the Woods
South Sudbury, Massachusetts 01776

Heritage Plantation and Garden
Grove St.
Sandwich, Massachusetts 02563

Mount Auburn Cemetery
580 Mt. Auburn St.
Cambridge, Massachusetts 02138

Michigan Arboretum, Ford Motor Co.
Michigan Ave. and Southfield Rd.
Dearborn, Michigan 48121

University of Michigan Botanical
   Gardens, Matthei Gardens
1800 Dixboro Rd.
Ann Arbor, Michigan 48105

Eloise Butler Wild Flower Garden and
   Bird Sanctuary
c/o Board of Park Commissioners
250 S. Fourth St.
Minneapolis, Minnesota 55415

Cora Hartshorn Arboretum and Bird
   Sanctuary
Forest Drive
Short Hills, New Jersey 07078

Carlsbad Botanical and Zoological Park
Carlsbad, New Mexico 88220

Brooklyn Botanic Garden
1000 Washington Avenue
Brooklyn, New York 11225

George Landis Arboretum
Esperance, New York 12066

New York Botanical Garden
200th St. east of Webster Avenue
Bronx, New York 10458

Ward Pound Ridge Reservation, The
  Meyer Arboretum
Cross River, New York 10518

Biltmore House and Gardens
Asheville, North Carolina 28802

Coker Arboretum
University of North Carolina
Chapel Hill, North Carolina 27514

Dawes Arboretum
Route 5
Newark, Ohio 43055

Holden Arboretum
9500 Sperry Rd.
Mentor, Ohio 44060

R. A. Stranahan Arboretum
University of Toledo
33 Birkhead Place
Toledo, Ohio 43606

Peavy Arboretum
School of Forestry, Oregon State
  College
Corvallis, Oregon 97330

Bowman's Hill State Wildflower
  Preserve
Washington Crossing State Park
Rt. 32 River Rd.
Washington Crossing, Pennsylvania 18977

Reflection Riding
419 Hermitage Avenue
Lookout Mountain, Tennessee 37350

Southwestern Arboretum
Southwestern College of Memphis
Memphis, Tennessee 38117

Point Defiance Park
Tacoma, Washington 98400

South King County Arboretum
  Foundation
Box 32
Kent, Washington 98031

West Virginia University Arboretum
Department of Biology
West Virginia University
Morgantown, West Virginia 26506

Conservation Groups

These organizations welcome participation by gardeners and non-gardeners alike. Write for further information.

The American Forestry Association
919 17th St. N.W.
Washington, D.C. 20006

Friends of the Earth
30 East 42nd St.
New York, N.Y. 10017

National Parks and Conservation Society
1701 18th St. N.W.
Washington, D.C. 20009

Sierra Club
1050 Mills Tower
San Francisco, Calif. 94104

The Wilderness Society
729 15th St. N.W.
Washington, D.C. 20005

California Tomorrow
681 Market St.
San Francisco, Calif. 94105

Agricultural Extension Service

This service is a combined effort of the county government, the state college or university responsible for agriculture, and the U. S. Department of Agriculture. Telephone numbers and addresses for these services will be found under the county government listings in your local telephone directories. The Agricultural Extension Service is the most up-to-date and extensive source of information on horticultural subjects in the United States. Circulars or bulletins answering frequently asked gardening questions are generally available in printed form for the asking. Addresses of these offices follow:

Auburn University
Auburn, Alabama 36830

College of Agriculture
University of Arizona
Tucson, Arizona 85721

University of Arkansas
Box 391
Little Rock, Arkansas 72203

Agricultural Extension Service
2200 University Avenue
Berkeley, California 94720

Colorado State University
Fort Collins, Colorado 80521

College of Agriculture
University of Connecticut
Storrs, Connecticut 06268

College of Agricultural Sciences
University of Delaware
Newark, Delaware 19711

University of Florida
217 Rolfs Hall
Gainsville, Florida 32601

College of Agriculture
University of Georgia
Athens, Georgia 30602

University of Hawaii
2500 Dole Street
Honolulu, Hawaii 96822

College of Agriculture
University of Idaho
Moscow, Idaho 83843

College of Agriculture
University of Illinois
Urbana, Illinois 61801

Agricultural Administration Building
Purdue University
Lafayette, Indiana 47907

Iowa State University
Ames, Iowa 50010

Kansas State University
Manhattan, Kansas 66502

College of Agriculture
University of Kentucky
Lexington, Kentucky 40506

Louisiana State University
Knapp Hall, University Station
Baton Rouge, Louisiana 70803

Department of Public Information
University of Maine
Orono, Maine 04473

University of Maryland
Agricultural Division
College Park, Maryland 20742

Stockbridge Hall
University of Massachusetts
Amherst, Massachusetts 01002

Department of Information Service
109 Agricultural Hall
East Lansing, Michigan 48823

Institute of Agriculture
University of Minnesota
St. Paul, Minnesota 55101

Mississippi State University
State College, Mississippi 39762

1-98 Agricultural Building
University of Missouri
Columbia, Missouri 65201

Offce of Information
Montana State University
Bozeman, Montana 59715

Department of Information
College of Agriculture
University of Nebraska
Lincoln, Nebraska 68503

Agricultural Communications Service
University of Nevada
Reno, Nevada 89507

Schofield Hall
University of New Hampshire
Durham, New Hampshire 03824

College of Agriculture
Rutgers, State University
New Brunswick, New Jersey 08903

New Mexico State University
Drawer 3A1
Las Cruces, New Mexico 88001

State College of Agriculture
Cornell University
Ithaca, New York 14850

North Carolina State University
State College Station
Raleigh, North Carolina 27607

North Dakota State University
State University Station
Fargo, North Dakota 58102

Ohio State University
2120 Fyffe Road
Columbus, Ohio 43210

Oklahoma State University
Stillwater, Oklahoma 74074

Oregon State University
206 Waldo Hall
Corvallis, Oregon 97331

Pennsylvania State University
Armsby Building
University Park, Pennsylvania 16802

University of Rhode Island
16 Woodwall Hall
Kingston, Rhode Island 02881

Clemson University
Clemson, South Carolina 29631

South Dakota State University
University Station
Brookings, South Dakota 57006

University of Tennessee
Box 1071
Knoxville, Tennessee 37901

Texas A & M University
Services Building
College Station, Texas 77843

Utah State University
Logan, Utah 84321

University of Vermont
Burlington, Vermont 05401

Virginia Polytechnic Institute
Blacksburg, Virginia 24061

Washington State University
115 Wilson Hall
Pullman, Washington 99163

West Virginia University
Evansdale Campus
Appalachian Center
Morgantown, West Virginia 26506

University of Wisconsin
Madison, Wisconsin 53706

University of Wyoming
Box 3354
Laramie, Wyoming 82070

Federal Extension Service
U. S. Department of Agriculture
Washington, D.C. 20250